Canning Meat Cookbook for Beginners

Unlock 1200 Days of Irresistible and Wallet-Friendly Recipes.
Master the Art of Safely Preserving Your Meat and Keep Your Pantry Stocked with Flavorful Delights.

EMMA YODER

EMMA YODER

EMMA YODER

EMMA YODER

CONTENTS

CANNING MEAT COOKBOOK FOR BEGINNERS

Introduction To Canning

History of Canning Food

In the long tradition of food preservation, canning is a relatively new phenomenon. Since before recorded history, humans have dried, salted, and fermented foods. However, heat-treating food and sealing it in airtight containers did not become popular until the late 18th century.

Napoleon Bonaparte offered a prize 1795 to anyone who could create a safe, dependable food preservation technique for his continuously marching army. Nicholas Appert took on the problem and devised a technique that entailed heat-processing food in glass jars strengthened with wire and sealing them with wax some 15 years later. That final approach is comparable to the one used by some individuals to seal jelly jars using paraffin wax (which, FYI, is no longer deemed safe).

The next innovation was the first actual "canning" procedure (as opposed to "bottling" or "jarring"). Englishman Peter Durand invented a technique for sealing food in "unbreakable" tin cans around 1810. In 1912, Thomas Kensett founded the first commercial canning enterprise in the United States.

Louis Pasteur clarified how the proliferation of germs causes food to deteriorate more than a century after Nicholas Appert accepted Napoleon's food preservation challenge. People previously understood that canning techniques worked, but not why.

Coincident with these developments, glass food preservation jars with metal clamps and interchangeable rubber rings were developed around the time of the American Civil War. These jars are still available, albeit they are now used for storing dry products rather than canning.

In 1858, John Mason invented a glass jar with a rubber seal and a threaded lid that screws on. Lightning and Atlas jars, two brands of wire-clamped jars that were popular from the late 1800s through the early 1960s, may sometimes be found at junkyards and thrift stores.

Why Canning Meat?

Canning meat has several benefits, making it a popular choice among many. Some of the reasons why people choose to can meat are as follows:

- **Food security and emergency preparedness:** Meat is often included in emergency food stores. When access to fresh food is limited due to natural disasters, power outages, or other circumstances, having a stockpile of canned meat on hand may provide sustenance. It offers a steady source of Protein and may aid in ensuring overall food security during challenging times.

- **Long Shelf Life:** Canning beef extends its shelf life significantly. Properly preserved meat may last for one to five years, or even longer, depending on the kind of meat and the canning procedure employed. Consequently, it's an excellent solution for long-term food preservation, emergency preparedness, or when fresh meat is in short supply.

- **Convenience:** Canned beef provides a fast and convenient source of protein. It eliminates the need for refrigeration or freezing, allowing you to have a Protein option in your cupboard. Canned meat may be easily incorporated into various dishes, including stews, soups, sandwiches, and casseroles, making supper preparation quick and simple.

- **Nutritional Value:** Canned beef retains its nutritional value. It contains essential macronutrients, including protein, vitamins (particularly B vitamins), and minerals (such as iron and zinc). Canning preserves these nutrients, making canned meat a valuable source of nutrition even when fresh meat is unavailable.

- **Savings:** Canning meat is a frugal method to stock up on meat during bargains, bulk buys, or seasonal discounts. You may save money and stock up on canned meat by buying larger quantities while prices are lower.

- **Food Preservation:** Canning meat aids in the prevention of food waste and deterioration. Bacteria, mold, and other germs that cause spoilage are decreased by storing meat in airtight containers. This allows you to safely store and preserve meat for an extended period, reducing the possibility of waste.

- **Reduced food waste:** Food waste is decreased because canning meat allows you to keep excess or leftover meat that would otherwise be thrown away. Rather than throwing away or allowing the meat to spoil, preserving it ensures that it may be used later, reducing food waste and saving money.

- **Cooking versatility:** Canned meat may be used in various recipes and dishes. It may be used in stews, soups, casseroles, sandwiches, and other dishes for a fast and simple Protein boost.

Canned meats such as chicken, tuna, and salmon are particularly popular owing to their versatility and ability to be used in various cuisines.

- **Taste and texture:** Canned meat retains its taste and texture nicely. The canning procedure helps preserve the meat's flavors and textures, allowing it to be enjoyed even after lengthy storage periods.

It is important to note that certain canning techniques and guidelines must be followed to ensure the safety and quality of preserved meat. Individuals may reap the benefits of preserving meat while ensuring food safety by following recommended techniques and using authorized recipes.

How to Start Canning Meat

One of the easiest and most versatile ways to store meat out of the fridge is to can it. Learn how to can beef, hog, poultry, venison, and other meats at home. Canning meat at home ensures you always have shelf-stable, ready-to-eat protein.

The meat in your freezer won't spoil if the power goes out, and you won't have to defrost it first. Although it's ideal if you cook it first, in a hurry, you may even consume canned beef directly from the jar with a fork.

After pressure canning, low-quality, rough slices become soft and tasty. They seem like they've been gently braising all day. This cookbook is a beginner's guide to canning meat, covering the necessary equipment, the canning method, and important safety precautions.

Safety Precautions

To ensure food safety, meat must be canned correctly. Here are a few reminders on safety:

- **Use the proper tools:** Canning jars, lids, and bands will all be needed. Check the jars and equipment for cracks, chips, or other faults that might compromise the seal.
- **Use tried-and-true canning recipes:** These recipes have been demonstrated to eliminate harmful germs when processed for the appropriate time and temperature. The USDA, NCHFP, and well-known canning periodicals are good places to get canned food ideas.
- **Follow the processing times and temperatures recommended:** Follow the canning recipe's instructions for processing times and temperatures. Botulism-causing Clostridium

botulinum must be eliminated by processing times and temperatures. Canning meat may be dangerous because of improper processing.

- **Use proper canning techniques:** The most common are pressure and boiling-water canning. Pressure-canned beef kills bacteria. It is risky to boil the meat for canning.

- **Avoid Canning Bad Meat:** Check for deterioration before canning meat. Throw aside discolored or slimy meat.

- **Prepare the meat correctly:** Ensure that the meat you're canning is fresh, of excellent quality, and properly handled. Trim the fat, remove bones, and slice meat into appropriate pieces according to the canning technique.

- **Brine Wild Meats before Canning:** To guarantee safe eating, can wild wildlife? Before canning, immerse strong-flavored wild foods in brine. This will destroy microorganisms and reduce the meat's gamey taste. To make brine, combine 1 cup of salt with 1 gallon of water. Before canning, immerse the meat in the solution for 24 hours.

- **Removing excess fat:** Removing excess fat may make the meat taste better. Fat removal helps the meat cook evenly. The fat dissolves while cooking, making meat uneven and spotty. Trimming fat before canning might improve consistency.

- **Remove Large Bones:** Breaking bones while canning might contaminate the meat, so remove them beforehand. Large bones may also make it hard to shut jars, allowing germs to infect food.

- **Store properly:** Store canned meat in a cool, dark area at a constant temperature. Begin with the oldest jar and name it.

- **Under pressure canning: Use a secure pressure canner and adhere to the instructions provided by the manufacturer.** Maintaining constant pressure during cooking ensures the meat reaches the right temperature.

- **Inspect jars and seals:** After complete processing, inspect jars and seals for good sealing. The lids should be concave and not burst when pressed. If jars fail to seal, refrigerate and consume the meat immediately.

These safeguards lower the risk of foodborne illness while ensuring safe, high-quality canned meat. These are general instructions; see respected canning sources for specific meat preservation procedures.

Equipment and Supplies Needed

Regarding meat canning, having the correct equipment and supplies is critical to ensuring safe and effective processing and preservation.

Here is a list of essential meat canning equipment and supplies:

- **Canner:** A big pot or vessel used to prepare and preserve canned meat by sterilizing it with heat.
- **Canning jars:** Glass containers designed specifically for canning meat, with an airtight seal to preserve the food for long periods.
- **Canning Lids and Bands:** Metal lids and screw bands fasten canning jars and create a vacuum seal that prevents bacterial contamination.
- **Jar Lifter:** A specialized gadget with grasping tongs used during the canning process to handle hot canning jars properly.
- **Food Mill or Victorio Strainer:** A food mill, also known as a Victorio strainer, is a culinary appliance that is used to purée or filter cooked meat, assuring a smooth texture and eliminating any undesired particles.
- **Wide Mouth Funnel:** A mouth, funnel-shaped device that puts meat and other ingredients into canning jars without spilling or making a mess.

Understanding The Canning Process

Pressure Canning

Pressure canning is the only safe method for preserving low-acid foods (those with a pH level higher than 4.6). Every kind of fruit, vegetable, meat, poultry, and seafood is included. Due to the potential for botulism, these foods must be canned using a pressure canner. The food is sealed in jars and placed in a pressure canner with 2 to 3 inches of water heated to 240 degrees Fahrenheit. You can't get to that temperature without using a pressure canner. Higher temperatures are required to kill hazardous microorganisms, such as Clostridium botulinum, which may cause botulism.

The following are the stages involved in pressure canning:

- **Prepare your canner:** Make sure your pressure canner is clean and in excellent operating order. Check the seals, vents, and safety features as directed by the manufacturer.
- Make the jars: Hot soapy water should be used to clean the canning jars, lids, and bands. Thoroughly rinse them.
- **Make the food:** Wash, peel, cut, or prepare the food to be canned.
- Fill the jars: Fill the jars with the prepared food, providing the headspace as recommended in the canning recipe.
- **Add liquid (if required):** Fill the jars with a predetermined quantity of liquid, such as water, broth, or syrup, if the recipe specifies it.
- **Jars should be sealed:** Once the rims have been wiped off, place the lids on top and tighten the bands with your fingers.
- **Load the canner:** Fill the pressure canner with the required quantity of water and put the filled jars inside using a jar lifter.

- **Vent the canner:** Follow the manufacturer's directions to vent the canner and remove any trapped air.
- **Prepare the jars:** Close the canner lid tightly and proceed as directed to bring the canner up to the appropriate pressure. Maintain the pressure for the duration specified in the recipe.
- **Cool and remove the jars:** Once the processing period is complete, turn off the heat and decrease the pressure naturally. Remove the jars carefully from the canner and lay them on a towel-lined surface. Allow them to cool completely.
- **Double-check the seals:** Once the jars have cooled, push down on the center of each lid to verify the seals. The jar is adequately sealed if it does not bend. If it flexes, refrigerate and eat the contents within a few days or reprocess the jar.

Water Bath Canning

Water bath canning is an excellent method for preserving high-acid goods such as fruits, jellies, jams, tomatoes, and pickles. These foods' inherent acidity inhibits the development of dangerous germs and makes them safe to prepare with boiling water.

The following are the stages involved in water bath canning:

- **Prepare your canner as follows:** Fill a big saucepan or water bath canner halfway with water, just enough to cover the jars by 1 to 2 inches. To avoid direct contact with the pot's bottom, use a rack at the bottom.
- **Prepare the food and jars:** Clean the jars, lids, and bands well. Fill the jars with the prepared meal, allowing enough headspace.
- **Jars should be sealed:** Once the rims have been wiped off, place the lids on top and tighten the bands with your fingers.
- **Load the canner:** Carefully insert the filled jars into the canner, ensuring they are completely immersed.
- **Process the jars:** Before filling the jars, bring the water to a gentle boil. Follow the recipe's instructions for the required processing time, starting the timer once the water hits a rolling boil.
- **Allow to cool before removing the jars:** Turn off the heat and let the jars sit in the canner for a few minutes once processing is complete. Using the jar lifter, take the jars out of the canner and set them over a towel-lined surface to cool.

- **Double-check the seals:** Once the jars have cooled, push down on the center of each lid to verify the seals. **The jar is adequately sealed if it does not bend.** If it flexes, refrigerate and eat the contents within a few days or reprocess the jar.

Differences between Raw Pack and Hot Pack

If you are new to the terms of the raw pack and hot pack, then it's important to know the science behind these canning/preserving methods. Raw and hot packs are canning techniques widely used to preserve food.
Both techniques help kill bacteria and avoid food spoilage. Now let us look at the difference between these two methods.

Raw Pack Canning

Raw pack canning, or a raw or cold pack, is packing raw or uncooked food straight into clean, sterilized jars without pre-cooking. The jars are filled with hot liquid, such as water, broth, or syrup, leaving the appropriate headspace. The jars are then processed in a pressure canner, heated to a high temperature to kill bacteria and create a vacuum seal.

The following stages are commonly included in the process:
- **Make the food:** Fruits and vegetables should be washed, peeled, and sliced.
- **Fill the jars:** Fill sterilized jars securely with raw food, leaving the required headspace (space at the top of the jar).
- **Add liquid:** If required, add hot water, syrup, juice, or recipe liquid to cover the meal and fill the headspace.
- **Remove air bubbles:** To remove air bubbles, run a non-metallic spatula or knife down the interior of the jar.
- **Apply lids:** Place sterilized lids on top of the metal bands and tighten until fingertip tight.
- **Filling the jars:** The jars should be filled and processed in a boiling water bath or pressure canner as per the manufacturer's instructions.
- **Cool and store:** Once the jars have been processed, take them from the canner, let them cool, and inspect them for appropriate sealing. Keep it in a cool, dark area.

Hot Pack Canning

Hot Pack Canning is the process of pre-cooking food before packing it into jars. The food is heated until it is hot and then packed into jars while still hot. The jars are filled with hot liquid, leaving the appropriate headspace, and processed in a canner. This method is one of the best ways to remove air and is preferred for foods processed in a boiling-water canner.

When you are done with the hot pack method for canning food, the color of foods looks not better than that of raw-packed foods, but within a short period, as it's safely stored, its color and taste are much superior then raw/cold pack food.

Important Notes:

Whether you are using a cold or hot pack, juices, syrups, or water added to the food should also be heated until boiled before adding to the jars. This method helps extend food's shelf life by shrinking it, removing air from food tissues, increasing the vacuum in sealed jars, and preventing food from floating.

The following are the major stages in hot pack canning:

- **Make the food:** Fruits and vegetables should be washed, peeled, and sliced. Cook your meats completely.
- **Heat the food:** Depending on the recipe, place the prepared food in a saucepan or pot and heat it until it is partly cooked.
- **Fill the jars**: Fill sterilized jars with hot food, leaving the required headspace.
- **Add liquid:** Add hot water, broth, syrup, or juice as needed to cover the meal and fill the headspace.
- **Remove air bubbles:** Slide a non-metallic spatula or knife around the jar's interior to remove air bubbles.
- **Apply lids:** Place sterilized lids on top of the metal bands and tighten until fingertip tight.
- **Canning:** Canning the jars in a boiling water bath or pressure canner according to the particular instructions for the canned food.
- **Cool and store:** Once the jars have been processed, take them from the canner, allow them to cool, and inspect them for appropriate sealing. Keep it in a cool, dark area.

Tips for Successful Canning

Canning meat is an effective method of long-term food preservation. For safe and delicious canned meat, consider these pointers.:

- Fresh, high-quality meat should be the first ingredient. Select the leanest pieces with no signs of deterioration or discoloration.

- Ensure all your canning equipment, including jars, lids, and canning utensils, is clean and prepared. Check the containers for chips and cracks; remove the broken ones.

- Utilize an authentic recipe that has been tested and proven. Adherence to the recipe is critical for a risk-free processing environment and to avoid the introduction of microorganisms that might be dangerous.

- When handling raw meat, keep your hands clean to avoid contaminating other food items. The meat should be refrigerated until it is time to can so that microbial development is inhibited.

- The risk of undercooking is minimized, and the heat may be evenly distributed if the meat is cooked beforehand. Roasting, boiling, or pressing the meat may be done in phases.

- Leave the correct headspace in the jars, as the recipe directs. This extra room facilitates processing growth and helps make a vacuum seal.

- After filling the jars, use a non-metallic device, such as a plastic spatula or bubble removal tool, to release any air bubbles trapped around the jar's rim.

- Wash the jars' rims before replacing the lids to ensure a proper seal. Follow the manufacturer's directions and use clean, new lids to get the job done.

- Meat is a low-acid product. It has to be prepared in a pressure canner and kept in pressure can jars. The manufacturer determines canner operating and processing times depending on jar size and altitude.

- Allow the canned meat to cool naturally after processing and pressure have been released, then store it. Please ensure the jars are sealed well, remove the bands, and put them somewhere cold and dark. Properly sealed jars may keep their contents fresh for a year or longer.

It's important to be careful and follow all canning guidelines while preserving meat. Always emphasize proper food handling to reduce the risk of food poisoning. Talk to a specialist in the field of food safety if you have any doubts or queries about canning.

Selecting And Preparing Meat

Choosing the Right Cuts: When it comes to meat canning, choosing the correct cuts is critical to producing a high-quality, tasty final result. Here are some important considerations to consider when selecting beef slices for canning:

- **Select tender beef cuts** such as sirloin, ribeye, or tenderloin. Because these slices have less connective tissue, they are more sensitive and delightful to consume after canning.
- Look for cuts that include marbling, which refers to intramuscular fat inside the meat. Marbled cuts, such as ribeye or chuck, provide more luscious and aromatic canned meat.
- **Consider the amount of fat in each piece.** A reasonable quantity of fat is preferred since it enhances the taste and moisture of the canned meat. Excess fat may result in a greasy final product.
- **Select cuts that have the same size and thickness.** This provides uniform cooking and consistency in the canned meat.
- **Choose cuts that may be utilized in several recipes.** Versatile cuts like chuck or shoulder may be utilized in stews, soups, or sandwiches, giving you more options for dinner preparation.
- Before canning, remember to trim any extra fat and remove any silver skin or stiff membranes from the cuts. Properly selected cuts will add to a lump of tasty and delightful canned meat that may be enjoyed over time.

Trimming and Cutting: Trimming and chopping meat for canning is critical in ensuring the canned meat's quality and safety. Here's a basic approach to trimming and cutting meat for canning:

- **Trim any excess fat from the meat.** Fat may impact the quality and shelf life of canned meat. If desired, leave a thin coating of fat on top for taste.
- **Remove any gristle, tendons, or tough connective tissue.** When canned, they may become tough and chewy.
- If using bone-in meat, gently remove the major bones to guarantee good meat canning.

- Determine the size of the canning jars or containers you will be using, and then cut the meat into pieces accordingly. Check that the pieces will fit inside the jars with some headroom.
- For more even cooking and a more consistent texture, cut the meat into equal pieces. This ensures that all components cook at the same pace throughout the canning process.

Trimming and cutting procedures may vary significantly based on the sort of meat and the canning recipe you're using, so check a trustworthy canning book or recipe for details.

Pre-cooking Techniques

Pre-cooking meat before canning is important in ensuring food safety and preservation. Here are various meat canning pre-cooking techniques:

- **Boiling:** Boiling meat in water or broth until thoroughly cooked kills unwanted germs and reduces the chance of spoiling during the canning process.
- **Roasting:** Roasting meat in the oven until it reaches a safe internal temperature not only adds taste but also aids in eliminating microorganisms and ensures proper cooking.
- **Braising:** Braising is browning meat in a skillet and then gently cooking it in liquid until soft. This procedure adds taste and aids in breaking down tough meat portions.
- **Pressure cooking:** A pressure cooker comes in handy when canning low-acid meats. It lets you sterilize the meat and ensure safe canning by cooking it at high temperatures and pressures.

What Cannot Be Canned?

- **Dairy products:** Milk, cream, butter and other dairy products.
- **Grains:** Oats, wheat, barley, rice, bread, noodles, pasta, crackers, biscuits, and pie dough. Etc.
- **Fried foods:** Foods that are deep-fried or have a high fat content, such as French fries or fried chicken. Etc.
- **Eggs:** Whole eggs or dishes containing eggs.
- **Nuts:** Almonds, walnuts, peanuts, cashews and pine nuts. Etc.
- **Add-ins:** Cornstarch, tapioca, arrowroot, cornmeal, flour.

Tips and techniques for Meat Canning Storage and Shelf Life

Understanding the shelf life of canned meat and proper storage is critical for ensuring food safety and quality.

Here are some canned meat storage recommendations and techniques:

- **Cool, dark area:** Canned meat should be stored in a cold, dark area, such as a pantry or basement. Avoid places with high temperatures or direct sunshine since they may impair the canned meat's freshness.
- **Adequate ventilation:** Ensure enough airflow around the stored jars to avoid moisture accumulation and mold development. Avoid keeping jars in densely packed containers or sealed containers.
- **Labeling and rotation:** To monitor the shelf life of each jar, label it with the date of canning. To ensure freshness, use a first-in, first-out cycle, utilizing the oldest jars first.
- **Shelf life:** Canned meat has a shelf life of 1 to 5 years, depending on the kind of meat and canning process employed. Specific recommendations should be found in canning recipes or instructions.
- **Regular inspections:** Inspect the jars regularly for symptoms of spoiling, such as bulging lids, odd odors, or discoloration. If any jars show indications of rotting, throw them out right away.
- **Alternative:** If you are concerned about the shelf life of canned meat, you may freeze it for longer-term preservation. Transfer the meat to freezer-safe containers, providing enough headspace, and freeze.

Storage conditions for canned meat should always put quality and safety first. It's better to be safe than sorry when it comes to canned meat, so if you have doubts about the quality of a certain canned meat jar, discard it.

100 Pressure Canner Recipes

Note: For all the 100 recipes provided, follow the instructions provided with your pressure canner for safe and proper usage. Adjusting the pressure and processing time based on your specific canner model and altitude is essential, as it can affect the canning process. To accomplice this, we have given tables for each category to get references while canning.

Chicken/Poultry Recipes

The proper canning pressure depends on your elevation and the type of canner you have in hand.

Guide Table for Chicken /Turkey/ Poultry

Table 1. Recommended process time for **Chicken or Rabbit** in a dial-gauge pressure canner.

Style of Pack	Jar Size	Process Time	Canner Pressure (PSI) at Altitudes of		
			0- 2,000 ft	2,001 - 4,000 ft	4,001 - 6,000 ft
Hot and Raw Without Bones:	Pints	75 min	**11 lb**	12 lb	13 lb
	Quarts	90 min	**11**	12 lb	13 lb
Hot and Raw With Bones:	Pints	65 min	**11 lb**	12 lb	13 lb
	Quarts	75 min	**11**	12	13 lb

Table 2. Recommended process time for **Chicken or Rabbit** in a weighted-gauge pressure canner.

Style of Pack	Jar Size	Process Time	Canner Pressure (PSI) at Altitudes of	
			0 - 1,000 ft	Above 1,000 ft
Hot and Raw Without Bones	Pints	75 min	**10 lb**	15 lb
	Quarts	90	**10**	15
Hot and Raw With Bones	Pints	65 min	**10 lb**	15 lb
	Quarts	75	**10**	15

Chicken And Vegetable Soup

Yield: 8 Servings

Preparation Time: 40 -60 Minutes (Excluding Canning Time)

Ingredients:

- 4 pounds bone-in chicken thighs
- 10 cups water
- 3 small carrots, peeled and diced
- 1 cup celery stalks, diced
- 1 large white onion, chopped
- 5 cloves garlic, minced
- 1-2 bay leaves
- 1 teaspoon dried thyme
- Salt and black pepper to taste

Directions

1. Ensure all canning jars are cleaned by washing them in soapy hot water, rinsing them well, and allowing them to dry in the air.
2. Add the jars with lids to a large pot and cover them with hot water to pre-heat them.
3. Bring the water to a simmer of about 180 degrees F, and let the jars and lids sit for 10 minutes in simmering water.
4. Next, prepare the pressure canner according to the manufacturer's instructions.
5. Take a Dutch oven and combine the chicken pieces, water, carrots, celery stalks, onion, garlic, bay leaves, thyme, salt, and pepper.
6. Let the mixture boil over medium heat.
7. Skim off any foam at the top.
8. Lower the heat and simmer it for 50-60 minutes.
9. Till now, the Chicken has gotten tender.
10. Remove the chicken pieces and set aside for cooling
11. Next, remove the chicken meat from the bones and cut it into bite-sized pieces.
12. Discard the bones and skin.

13. Strain the soup and collect the vegetables and herbs in a bowl.

14. Simmer the strained soup again.

15. Add the chicken pieces, reserved herbs, and vegetables into the strained soup.

16. Simmer it for another 10 minutes.

17. Ladle this hot soup into the sterilized jars, ensuring 1-inch of headspace.

18. Stir and de-bubble the jars.

19. Wipe the rims with a damp cloth.

20. Put jar lids on top and tighten the bands until fingertip tight.

21. Place the jars inside your pressure canner and process the jars according to recommended time and pressure for altitude.

22. Once done, carefully remove the jars from the canner.

23. Let the jars cool completely.

24. Check the seal once jars are cooled off; they should not flex when pressed.

25. Store the jars properly in a cool and dark place

Nutrition Facts:

Calories: 451 | Total Fat: 16.9g | Saturated Fat: 4.6g | Sodium: 228mg

Carbohydrate 4.7g| Sugars 1.9g | Protein: 66.2g

.

Chicken Curry

Yield: 4 Servings

Preparation Time: 1 Hour (Excluding Canning Time)

Ingredients

- 3 tablespoons vegetable oil
- 2 small white onions, chopped
- 4 cloves of garlic, minced
- 4 teaspoon ginger, grated
- 2 tablespoons curry powder
- 1 teaspoon ground coriander
- 2 pounds of boneless and skinless chicken breasts cut into 1-inch pieces
- 1 cup tomatoes, diced
- 2 cups chicken broth
- 4 tablespoons tomato paste
- Salt and black pepper to taste

Directions

1. Take a large cooking pot and heat vegetable oil over medium heat.
2. Add in the chopped onions and sauté for 5 minutes.
3. Then add the garlic and ginger into the pot and cook for 1 minute until the aroma comes.
4. Now add the curry powder and coriander.
5. Cook until aroma comes.
6. Add the chicken pieces to the pot.
7. Cook until browned for about 6 minutes.
8. Next, add the diced tomatoes, chicken broth, and tomato paste.
9. Cook until combined.
10. Add salt and pepper.
11. Let it boil, and then reduce the heat.
12. Cover the pot and simmer for about 60 minutes.
13. Meanwhile, prepare your canning jars by sterilizing them properly.
14. Ladle the hot chicken curry into the sterilized jars, ensuring 1-inch headspace.
15. Stir and de-bubble the jars.
16. Wipe the rims of the jars.
17. Put the lids and tighten the band.
18. Process the jars in your pressure canner according to recommended time and pressure for specific altitudes and pressure canner types. Once done, carefully remove the jars from the canner.
19. Let the jars cool for 25 minutes.
20. Check the seals once the jars are cooled off.
21. Store the properly sealed jars in a cool, dark place.

Nutrition Facts

Calories: 508 | Total Fat: 18.5g | Saturated Fat: 4.3g | Sodium: 547mg

Carbohydrate: 12.6g | Sugars: 5.1g | Protein: 70.4g

Bourbon Chicken

Yield: 4 Servings

Preparation Time: 1 Hour (Excluding Canning Time)

Ingredients

- 2 tablespoons vegetable oil
- 2 pounds of Chicken, cubed into 1-inch pieces
- 2 cloves of crushed garlic
- 1 teaspoon crushed red pepper
- 1/4 cup apple juice
- 1/4 cup light brown sugar
- 2 tablespoons ketchup
- ½ tablespoon cider vinegar
- 1/2 cup water
- 1/3 cup soy sauce

Directions

1. Heat vegetable oil in a cooking pot over medium heat and stir-fry the Chicken until brown.
2. Combine all ingredients listed in the recipe and bring to a boil.
3. Meanwhile, prepare the jars by sterilizing them for proper canning.
4. Prepare the pressure canner according to the manufacturer's instructions.
5. Divide the prepared Chicken evenly into sterilized jars and pour the sauce on top.
6. If you do not have enough sauce, add water to the fill line, leaving 1-inch headspace.
7. Stir and de-bubble.
8. Clean the rims with a damp kitchen towel.
9. Place lids on top and seal jars tightly.
10. Process the jars in your pressure canner according to your altitude's recommended time and pressure.
11. Once done, carefully remove the jars from the canner.
12. Let the jars cool for 25 minutes.
13. Check the seals once the jars are cooled off.
14. Store the properly sealed jars in a cool, dark place.

Nutrition Facts

Calories: 464 | Total Fat: 13.8g | Saturated Fat: 3.3g | Sodium: 1429mg

Carbohydrate: 14.4g | Sugars: 12.4g | Protein: 67.3g

Greek Chicken

Yield: 20-25 Servings

Preparation Time: 60-75 Minutes (Excluding Canning Time)

Ingredients:

- 3 tablespoons of vegetable oil
- 14 pounds of Chicken thighs, 1-inch pieces and boneless
- 20 cloves Garlic, minced
- 10 tablespoons of Lemon juice, freshly squeezed
- Sea salt, as needed
- ½ cup Lemon pepper
- 4 tablespoons of fresh oregano
- 5 tablespoons of Dijon mustard
- Filtered water to top the jars

Directions

1. First, sterilize the canning jars well.
2. Heat oil in a cooking pot over medium heat and cook the Chicken until brown.
3. Prepare the pressure canner as per instructions on canners by manufacturers.
4. Fill the jars with Chicken up to 1-1/2 from the top.
5. Add equally distributed garlic, lemon juice, salt, lemon juice, pepper, oregano, and Dijon mustard to each jar.
6. Fill the jars with warm filtered water the rest of the way to 1 -14 inch headspace.
7. Stir and remove the bubbles from the jars.
8. Clean the jar rims with a damp cloth.
9. Put the lids on the canning jars and tighten the band.
10. Process the jars in your pressure canner according to recommended time and pressure.
11. Once done, carefully remove the jars from the canner.
12. Let the jars cool completely.
13. Check the seals once the jars are cooled off.
14. Store the properly sealed jars in a cool, dark place.

Nutrition Facts

Calories: 605 | Total Fat: 24.7g | Saturated Fat: 6.7g | Sodium: 305mg

Carbohydrate: 2.4g | Sugars: 0.3g | Protein: 88.1g

Canned Rosemary Chicken

Yield: 20-25 Servings

Preparation Time: 45-65 Minutes (Excluding Canning Time)

Ingredients

- Sprigs fresh rosemary, as needed
- 10 pounds of boneless, skinless chicken breast cut into 1-inch pieces
- 1 salt, about 1 teaspoon per pint

Directions

1. Start by sterilizing the jars and lids for canning.
2. Prepare the pressure canner as per instructions on canners by manufacturers.
3. Place one sprig of rosemary at the bottom of the sterilized jar.
4. Now fill the jars with the Chicken, leaving about 1 -1/2 inches of headspace.
5. Add a sprig of rosemary on top of each jar.
6. Sprinkle 1 teaspoon of salt in each jar.
7. Tightly seal the jars.
8. Wipe the rim of each jar using a clean, damp towel to ensure a strong seal.
9. Tighten the lids and bands securely on each jar.
10. Process the jars in your pressure canner.
11. Processing time in the pressure canner may vary depending on your altitude.
12. Once done, carefully remove the jars from the canner.
13. Let the jars cool for 45 minutes.
14. Check the seals once the jars are cooled off.
15. Store the properly sealed jars in a cool, dark place.

Nutrition Facts

Calories: 259 | Total Fat: 5.7g | Saturated Fat: 0g | Sodium: 116mg

Carbohydrate: 0g | Sugars: 0g | Protein: 48.1g

Spicy Lime Chicken

Yield: 20-25 Servings

Preparation Time: 45-60 Minutes (Excluding Canning Time)

Ingredients

- 14 pounds of Chicken breast, cut into 1-inch pieces
- 16 teaspoons of chili lime seasoning
- 14 teaspoons of Jalapeño powder
- Sea salt, to taste
- Black pepper, to taste
- Filtered water to fill the jars

Directions

1. First, sterilize the canning jars and lids for canning.
2. Prepare the pressure canner with water as per instructions.
3. Do not heat the pressure canner.
4. Fill the canning jars with Chicken up to 1 -1/2 from the top.
5. Then top the jars with chili lime seasoning, jalapeno powder, salt, and pepper.
6. Stir and de-bubble, then fill the jars with filtered water up to 1-1/4 inch headspace.
7. Tightly seal the jars.
8. Wipe the rim of each jar using a clean, damp towel to ensure a strong seal.
9. Tighten the lids and bands securely on each jar.
10. Clean the rims with a clean damp kitchen towel.
11. Add the lids on the jars and tighten the band.
12. Now, add jars to the canner and process the canning jars in a pressure canner according to your altitude's recommended time and pressure.
13. Once done, carefully remove the jars from the canner.
14. Let the jars cool for 25 minutes.
15. Check the seals once the jars are cooled off.
16. Store the properly sealed jars in a cool, dark place.

Nutrition Facts

Calories: 302 | Total Fat: 6.6g | Saturated Fat: 0g | Sodium: 135mg

Carbohydrate: 10,1g | Sugars: 0g | Protein: 56.1g

Cream of Chicken and Mushroom Soup

Yield: 4 Servings

Preparation Time: 45 Minutes (Excluding Canning Time)

Ingredients

- 2 pounds Mushrooms, chopped (any kind)
- 2.5 pounds Chicken, ½ inch pieces
- 3 Stalk celery, chopped
- ½ large white onion, chopped fine
- 3 cloves garlic, crushed
- 1 teaspoon ground black pepper
- ½ teaspoon herbs de Provence
- ½ teaspoon dried parsley
- 8 cups chicken stock
- 1/2 cup Clear-Jell
- 1/2 cup cold water

Directions

1. Combine all main ingredients in a large Dutch oven.
2. Bring it to a boil.
3. Simmer for 15 minutes.
4. Whisk the slurry ingredients into a bowl and add to the hot soup.
5. Bring the soup again to a boil.
6. Sterilize the jars and lids for canning.
7. Prepare the pressure canner with water as per instruction, do not heat it.
8. Fill the hot canning jars, leaving 1 inch of headspace at the top.
9. Remove any bubbles inside the jars.
10. Clean the rim of each jar to ensure a proper seal.
11. Put a lid on each jar and secure it with a ring.
12. Carefully place the filled jars into a pressure canner.
13. Process the jars in your pressure canner according to recommended time and pressure for the type of canner and altitude of the area.
14. Once done, carefully remove the jars from the canner.
15. Let the jars cool for 25 minutes.
16. Check the seals once the jars are cooled off.
17. Store the properly sealed jars in a cool, dark place.

Nutrition Facts

Calories: 511 | Total Fat: 10.4g| Saturated Fat: 2.7g | Sodium: 1731mg

Carbohydrate: 12.1g | Sugars: 6.3g | Protein: 91.2g

Roasted Red Bell Pepper and Chicken Soup

Yield: 16 Servings

Preparation Time: 1 Hour 30 Minutes (Excluding Canning Time)

Ingredients

- 8 large red bell peppers, seedless and diced
- 4 teaspoons Olive oil, divided
- Cracked black pepper, divided and as needed
- Salt, divided and as needed
- 2 large white onions, diced
- 14 cloves Garlic, minced
- 20-22 ounces Sun-dried tomatoes packed in oil, drained
- 10-12 cups of Chicken broth
- 3 teaspoons Onion powder
- 3 teaspoons Garlic powder
- 2 Bay leaves, broken into quarters
- 8 pounds of Chicken breasts, diced into 1-inch pieces

Directions

1. Sterilize the jars and lids for canning.
2. Prepare the pressure canner as instructed, fill it with water, and simmer at low heat.
3. Add the red bell peppers, 2 teaspoons olive oil, black pepper, and salt in a large roasting or baking pan.
4. Bake it for 20 minutes.
5. In a Dutch oven, cook the onions, garlic, and remaining olive oil over low heat until soft.
6. Add the baked peppers and sun-dried tomatoes to the Dutch oven.
7. Mix it well.
8. Use a blender to puree this mixture.
9. Transfer it to the Dutch oven and pour the broth, onion powder, garlic powder, bay leaves, and salt.
10. Bring it to a boil, then cover and let it simmer for 10 minutes.
11. Add diced chicken to the prepared jars, filling them no more than half full.
12. Ladle the hot broth over the Chicken, leaving 1 inch of headspace.
13. Remove the bubbles from the jars.
14. Clean the rim of each jar to ensure a proper seal.
15. Put a lid on each jar and secure it with a ring.

16. Carefully place the filled jars into a pressure canner.

17. Process the jars in your pressure canner according to your altitude's recommended time and pressure.

18. Once done, carefully remove the jars from the canner.

19. Let the jars cool for 20 minutes.

20. Check the seals once the jars are cooled off.

21. Store the properly sealed jars in a cool, dark place.

Nutrition Facts

Calories: 574 | Total Fat: 24g | Saturated Fat: 5.7g | Sodium: 781mg

Carbohydrate: 16.7g | Sugars: 4.6g | Protein: 71.6g

Aromatic Spiced Chicken

Yield: 20 Servings

Preparation Time: 1 Hour 30 Minutes (Excluding Canning Time)

Ingredients

- 12 cups Chicken broth
- 3/4 cup Soy sauce
- 2 teaspoons Onion powder
- 2 teaspoons Garlic powder
- 1-inch ginger, grated
- 1/4 teaspoon Cayenne pepper
- 10 pounds of Chicken, diced into 1-inch pieces
- 3 large onions, chopped
- 6 carrots, diced
- 8-15 Cloves garlic, minced

Directions

1. Prepare the pressure canner as instructed, fill it with water, and simmer at low heat.
2. Add the chicken broth, soy sauce, onion powder, garlic powder, ginger, and cayenne pepper, in a Dutch oven over medium heat, and combine.
3. Let the boil come, reduce the heat, and simmer it for 10 minutes.
4. Divide the diced Chicken, onions, and carrots evenly amongst the Jars.
5. Divide minced cloves of garlic into each jar.
6. Fill the jars with the broth, leaving 1-inch of headspace.
7. Remove the bubbles from the jars.
8. Clean the rim of each jar to ensure a proper seal.
9. Put a lid on each jar and secure it with a ring.
10. Carefully place the filled jars into a pressure canner.
11. Process the jars according to your altitude's recommended time and pressure.
12. Once done, carefully remove the jars from the canner.
13. Let the jars cool for 25 minutes.
14. Check the seals once the jars are cooled off.
15. Store the properly sealed jars in a cool, dark place.

Nutrition Facts: Calories: 391 | Total Fat: 7.7g | Saturated Fat: 2.2g | Sodium: 1154mg
Carbohydrate: 6g | Sugars: 2.6g | Protein: 69.8g

Chicken Piccata

Yield: 16-26 Servings

Preparation Time: 1 Hour 30 Minutes (Excluding Canning Time)

Ingredients

- 12-14 pounds of Chicken breast, cut into 2-inch cubes
- 6 Shallots, minced
- 14 cloves Garlic, minced
- 15 tablespoons of Lemon juice, fresh
- 1/2 cup Capers, drained
- 3 -1/2 teaspoon sea salt
- 4 teaspoons of fresh cracked black pepper
- Filtered water for topping the jars

Directions

1. Sterilize the jars and lids for canning.
2. Prepare the pressure canner with water as per instructions, do not heat it.
3. Fill the prepared jars with Chicken up to 1 -1/2 from the top.
4. Fill each jar with shallot, clove, minced garlic, lemon juice, capers, salt, and pepper.
5. The amount should be equally divided between the jars.
6. Fill with filtered water and remove the bubbles, if any.
7. Clean the rim of each jar to ensure a proper seal.
8. Put a lid on each jar and secure it with a ring.
9. Carefully place the filled jars into a pressure canner.
10. Process the jars in your pressure canner according to your altitude's recommended time and pressure.
11. Once done, carefully remove the jars from the canner.
12. Let the jars cool for 15 minutes.
13. Check the seals once the jars are cooled off.
14. Store the properly sealed jars in a cool, dark place.

Nutrition Facts

Calories: 398 | Total Fat: 8.7g | Saturated Fat: 0.1 | Sodium: 655mg

Carbohydrate: 1.7g | Sugars: 0.4g | Protein: 72.6

Chicken Medley

Yield: 10 Servings

Preparation Time: 45 Minutes (Excluding Canning Time)

Ingredients

- 18 cups chicken broth
- 5 cloves garlic, crushed
- 1/2 teaspoon onion powder
- Ground black pepper, to taste
- 2 teaspoons dried parsley
- 5 pounds of chicken breast, cut into 1-inch cubes
- 1 white and large onion, diced
- 1 pound of mushrooms, cleaned and sliced or chunked
- 12 ounces of pimientos, diced

Directions

1. Sterilize the jars and lids for canning.
2. Prepare the pressure canner with water as instructed; add the water to the canner to a low simmer.
3. In a large pot, add the chicken broth, garlic, onion powder, pepper, and parsley. Bring to a boil and simmer at low for 10 minutes.
4. Divide the Chicken into the sterilized jars. Top each jar with an equally distributed amount of onions, mushrooms, and pimientos.
5. Fill jars with broth leaving 1-inch headspace.
6. Remove any bubbles from the jars.
7. Clean the rim of each jar to ensure a proper seal.
8. Put a lid on each jar and secure it with a ring.
9. Carefully place the filled jars into a pressure canner.
10. Process the jars in your pressure canner according to your altitude's recommended time and pressure.
11. Once done, carefully remove the jars from the canner.
12. Let the jars cool for 15 minutes.
13. Check the seals once the jars are cooled off.
14. Store the properly sealed jars in a cool, dark place.

Nutrition Facts

Calories: 386 | Total Fat: 8.6g | Saturated Fat: 0.7g | Sodium: 1496mg

Carbohydrate: 14.7g | Sugars: 9.3g | Protein: 59.8g

Chicken And Gravy

Yield: 4 Servings

Preparation Time: 45 Minutes (Excluding Canning Time)

Ingredients

- 1 cup of chopped onions
- 1 cup of chopped celery
- 1 cup of potato, peeled, diced
- 2 pounds of Chicken, boneless
- 2 teaspoons salt
- 2 teaspoons poultry seasoning
- 1 teaspoon black pepper, ground
- 4 tablespoons dry white wine
- Hot chicken broth, as needed, to fill the jars

Directions

1. Add all the ingredients to a large bowl.
2. Mix all the ingredients well with the spoon.
3. The jar size choice is up to you.
4. Sterilize the jars and lids for canning.
5. Pack the hot jars firmly with the mixture.
6. Leave 1-inch of headspace.
7. Top up the jars with hot broth.
8. Remove any bubbles and adjust the headspace.
9. Clean the rim of each jar to ensure a proper seal.
10. Put a lid on each jar and secure it with a ring.
11. Carefully place the filled jars into a pressure canner.
12. Process the jars in your pressure canner according to your altitude's recommended time and pressure.
13. Once done, carefully remove the jars from the canner.
14. Let the jars cool for 15 minutes.
15. Check the seals once the jars are cooled off.
16. Store the properly sealed jars in a cool, dark.

Nutrition Facts: Calories: 388 | Total Fat: 7g | Saturated Fat: 2g | Sodium: 1329mg
Carbohydrate: 8g | Sugars: 1.9g | Protein: 66.7g

Sweet and Sour Chicken

Yield: 8-10 Servings

Preparation Time: 45 Minutes (Excluding Canning Time)

Ingredients

- 3/4 cup brown sugar
- 1/4 cups white vinegar
- 12 teaspoons soy sauce
- 8 teaspoons ketchup
- 1 teaspoon of ginger powder
- 3 (20 ounces cans) pineapple chunks drained, reserve the juice
- Filtered water
- 5 pounds of chicken breasts cut into 1-inch bite-sized pieces
- 2 onions chopped
- 2 large green peppers chopped
- 1 large red pepper chopped

Directions

1. Process your canner according to the manufacturer's instructions.
2. Add the brown sugar, vinegar, soy sauce, ketchup, ginger, 2 1/2 cups of pineapple juice, and half a cup of water in a pot and boil at low heat until the sugar has dissolved.
3. Add the Chicken, onions, green and red peppers, and pineapple into prepared jars, ensuring 1-1/2 inches of head space.
4. Pour pot liquid into each jar.
5. Remove any bubbles and ensure 1-inch head space.
6. Clean the rim of each jar to ensure a proper seal.
7. Put a lid on each jar and secure it with a ring.
8. Carefully place the filled jars into a pressure canner.
9. Process the jars in pressure canner according to your altitude's recommended time and pressure.
10. Once done, carefully remove the jars from the canner.
11. Let the jars cool completely.
12. Check the seals once the jars are cooled off.
13. Store the properly sealed jars in a cool, dark.

Nutrition Facts: Calories: 608 | Total Fat: 21g | Saturated Fat: 5.8g

Carbohydrate: 16.1g | Sugars: 15g | Protein: 82.7g

Canned Taco Chicken

Yield: 24 Servings

Preparation Time: 35 Minutes (Excluding Canning Time)

Ingredients

- 14 pounds of Chicken, 1 -1/2 inch diced
- 1 white and large onion, diced
- 4 poblano peppers, roasted, peeled, seeded, and diced
- 3 teaspoons kosher salt
- 6 teaspoons garlic powder
- 2 teaspoons ground cumin
- 4 teaspoons onion powder
- 6 teaspoons chili powder
- 4 teaspoons Mexican oregano
- 1 tablespoon cayenne pepper
- Filtered water, cold to top the jar off

Directions

1. Sterilize the jars and lids for canning.
2. Prepare the pressure canner with water as per instructions.
3. Add Chicken to a large bowl with all the listed ingredients excluding water.
4. Coat the Chicken well and pack the Chicken into jars, leaving 1-inch headspace.
5. Remove any bubbles, leaving 1-1/2 inches of head space.
6. Add cold water to each jar; maintain 1-inch of head space.
7. Clean the rim of each jar.
8. Put a lid on each jar and secure it with a ring.
9. Carefully place the filled jars into a pressure canner.
10. Process the jars in your pressure canner according to your altitude's recommended time and pressure.
11. Next, carefully remove the jars from the canner.
12. Let the jars cool for 10-15 minutes.
13. Check the seals once the jars are cooled off.
14. Store the properly sealed jars in a cool, dark.

Nutrition Facts: Calories: 410 | Total Fat: 8.3g | Saturated Fat: 2.3g | Sodium: 465mg Carbohydrate: 2.3g | Sugars: 0.8g | Protein: 77.2g

Chicken Delight

Yield: 15 Servings

Preparation Time: 45 Minutes (Excluding Canning Time)

Ingredients

- 6 1/2 cups chicken broth
- 6- 1/2 cups apple cider
- 2 cups apple brandy
- 1/4 cup Dijon mustard
- 1 tablespoon kosher salt
- 6-7 gala apples, peeled and wedged
- 2 onions, sliced
- 7 pounds of chicken thighs, boneless, skinless, cubed
- 14 cloves garlic, minced
- 6 sprigs of fresh thyme

Directions

1. Sterilize the jars and lids for canning.
2. Prepare the pressure canner with water per instructions bringing water to a low simmer.
3. Add the broth, cider, brandy, onion powder, Dijon, salt, apples, and onions into a Dutch oven.
4. Let it boil and turn the heat low, cover and simmer for 15 minutes.
5. Add an equally distributed amount of chicken, garlic, and thyme to the sterilized jars, ensuring 1-1/2 inches of head space.
6. Pour the broth into jars, leaving 1-inch headspace.
7. Remove any bubbles and clean the rim of each jar and de-bubble.
8. Put a lid on each jar and secure it with a ring.
9. Carefully place the filled jars into a pressure canner.
10. Process the jars in your pressure canner according to your altitude's recommended time and pressure.
11. Next, carefully remove the jars from the canner.
12. Let the jars cool for 10-15 minutes.
13. Check the seals once the jars are cooled off.
14. Store the properly sealed jars in a cool, dark.

Nutrition Facts: Calories: 530 | Total Fat: 16.8g | Saturated Fat: 4.5g | Sodium: 1060mg
Carbohydrate: 26.6g | Sugars: 21.5g | Protein: 64g

Chicken Paprika

Yield: 20 Servings

Preparation Time: 35 Minutes (Excluding Canning Time)

Ingredients

- 12 cups chicken broth
- 28 ounces of diced tomatoes, canned
- 15 cloves garlic, minced
- 2 teaspoons onion powder
- 2 teaspoons garlic powder
- Canning salt, as needed
- 16 teaspoons of sweet paprika powder
- 10 pounds of Chicken, cut into 1- 1/2-inch chunks
- 2 white onions, chopped
- 2 green bell peppers, chopped

Directions

1. Sterilize the jars and lids for canning.
2. Prepare the pressure canner with water per instructions bringing water to a low simmer.
3. Now prepare the broth and for that, pour chicken broth and tomatoes into a Dutch oven and add garlic, onion powder, garlic powder, salt, and paprika powder.
4. Let it to a boil and simmer for about 10 minutes.
5. Meanwhile, prepare jars and fill each jar with the distributed amount of chicken, onion, and bell peppers, leaving 1-1/2 inches of head space.
6. Fill the jars with hot broth, ensuring 1-inch head space.
7. Remove bubbles.
8. For each jar, clean the rim, put a lid and secure it with a ring
9. Carefully place the filled jars into a pressure canner.
10. Process the jars in your pressure canner according to recommended time and pressure.
11. Next, carefully remove the jars from the canner.
12. Let the jars cool for 15 minutes.
13. Check the seals once the jars are cooled off.
14. Store the properly sealed jars in a cool, dark.

Nutrition Facts: Calories: 386 | Total Fat: 7.8g | Saturated Fat: 2.2g | Sodium: 604mg

Carbohydrate: 5.2g | Sugars: 2.7g | Protein: 69.4g

Turkey Leg

Yield: 5-10 Servings

Preparation Time: 45 Minutes (Excluding Canning Time)

Ingredients

- 10 Turkey legs
- Water, as needed to fill the jars
- Salt, as needed

Directions

1. Sterilize the jars and lids for canning.
2. Prepare the pressure canner with water per instructions.
3. Wash and clean the turkey legs thoroughly.
4. Add turkey legs, water, and salt to a large Dutch oven.
5. Partially cook the legs for 10 minutes (2/3 done).
6. Meanwhile, prepare the canning jars.
7. Sterilize the jars and lids for canning.
8. Place turkey legs into the sterilized jars, leaving about 1 -1/2 inch of headspace.
9. Ladle the pot of cooking liquid into the jars, covering the legs completely and leaving 1-inch of head space.
10. Wipe the rims of the jars so they seal properly.
11. Add the lids and rings on top of the jars, tightening the rings finger-tight.
12. Close and tightly seal the jars.
13. Carefully place the filled jars into a pressure canner.
14. Process the jars in your pressure canner according to your altitude's recommended time and pressure.
15. Next, carefully remove the jars from the canner.
16. Let the jars cool for 10-15 minutes.
17. Check the seals once the jars are cooled off.
18. Store the properly sealed jars in a cool, dark.

Nutrition Facts: Calories: 417 | Total Fat: 13.3g | Saturated Fat: 4.1g | Sodium: 212mg
Carbohydrate: 0g | Sugars: 0g | Protein: 69.8g

Spicy Buffalo Chicken Wings

Yield: 8 Servings

Preparation Time: 35 Minutes (Excluding Canning Time)

Ingredients

- 4 pounds of chicken wings
- 4 cups of water
- 1 cup of hot sauce
- Canning salt, as needed

Directions

1. Sterilize the jars and lids for canning.
2. Prepare the pressure canner as per the manufacturer's instructions.
3. Clean the chicken wings thoroughly under cold running water.
4. In a Dutch oven, combine water, hot sauce, and salt.
5. Put the chicken wings in the pot and let it boil.
6. Partially cook the wings for 10 minutes.
7. Sterilize the canning jars.
8. Equally, add wings to the jars and pour in the liquid at the bottom of the pot, leaving 1-inch head space.
9. Remove bubbles and wipe the rims of the jars so they seal properly.
10. Add the lids and rings to the jars, tightening the rings finger-tight.
11. Close and tightly seal the jars.
12. Carefully place the filled jars into a pressure canner.
13. Process the jars in your pressure canner according to your altitude's recommended time and pressure.
14. Next, carefully remove the jars from the canner.
15. Let the jars cool for 15 minutes.
16. Check the seals once the jars are cooled off.
17. Store the properly sealed jars in a cool, dark.

Nutrition Facts: Calories: 431 | Total Fat: 16.8g | Saturated Fat: 4.6g | Sodium: 195mg
Carbohydrate: 0g | Sugars: 0g | Protein: 65.6g

Honey Barbecue Chicken Wings

Yield: 8 Servings

Preparation Time: 30-35 Minutes (Excluding Canning Time)

Ingredients

- 4 pounds of chicken wings
- 4 cups of water
- 2 cups of barbecue sauce
- 1/2 cup of honey

Directions

1. Sterilize the jars and lids for canning.
2. Prepare the pressure canner as per the manufacturer's instructions.
3. The first step is cleaning the wings and washing them thoroughly under tap water.
4. Combine water, barbecue sauce, and honey to a large pot.
5. Next, add wings.
6. Simmer for 10 minutes until chicken wings are partially cooked.
7. Sterilize the jars and lids for canning.
8. Place wings from the pot into the sterilized jars, leaving about 1 -1/2 inch of headspace.
9. Spoon the pot of cooking liquid into the jars, covering the legs completely; maintain the 1-inch head space.
10. Wipe the rims of the jars so they seal properly.
11. Close and tightly seal the jars.
12. Carefully place the filled jars into a pressure canner.
13. Process the jars in your pressure canner according to your altitude's recommended time and pressure.
14. Next, carefully remove the jars from the canner.
15. Let the jars cool.
16. Check the seals once the jars are cooled off.
17. Store the properly sealed jars in a cool, dark.

Nutrition Facts: Calories: 589 | Total Fat: 17g | Saturated Fat: 4.6g | Sodium: 899mg
Carbohydrate: 40.1g | Sugars: 33.7g | Protein: 65.7g

Canned Goose

Yield: 20 Servings

Preparation Time: 30-60 Minutes (Excluding Canning Time)

Ingredients

- 10 pounds of goose breast pieces cut into 1-inch chunks
- 4 cups vegetable broth
- 2 medium white onions, sliced
- 4 cloves garlic, minced
- 2 teaspoons salt
- 1-1/2 teaspoon black pepper
- 2 teaspoons dried thyme
- 1 bay leaf

Directions

1. Sterilize the jars and lids for canning.
2. Prepare the pressure canner as per the manufacturer's instructions.
3. Wash and clean the goose breast pieces under tap water.
4. Add the goose, vegetable broth, onions, garlic, salt, black pepper, thyme, and bay leaf in a Dutch oven, and simmer.
5. Now cook the goose for 1 hour with the lid on.
6. Till now, the goose will be tender.
7. Remove the goose and set it aside to let it get cool.
8. Then cut the goose into bite-sized pieces.
9. Sterilized canning jars and put shredded meat in them, then left about 1 -1/2 inch of headspace.
10. Spoon the cooking liquid from the pot into the jar, ensuring 1-inch head space.
11. Remove any bubbles from the jars.
12. Make sure the meat is well covered.
13. Clean the jar rims, place the lids on top, and seal the jars.
14. Process the jars in a pressure canner filled with water according to your altitude's recommended time and pressure.
15. Once done, remove the jars and let them sit for 10 minutes to get cool.
16. Completely remove the jars from the canner, and let them cool.
17. Check the seals once the jars are cooled off.
18. Store the canning jars in a cool, dark place.

Nutrition Facts: Calories: 290 | Total Fat: 9.4g | Saturated Fat: 0.1g | Sodium: 386mg Carbohydrate: 1.5g | Sugars: 0.6g | Protein: 53.7g

Fish Recipes

Guide Table for Mackerel, Salmon, Trout, and other Fatty Fish except for Tuna

Table 1. Recommended process time for **Fish** in a dial-gauge pressure canner.						
			Canner Pressure (PSI) at Altitudes of			
Style of Pack	**Jar Size**	**Process Time**	**0 – 2,000 ft**	**2,001 - 4,000 ft**	**4,001 - 6,000 ft**	**6,001 - 8,000 ft**
Raw	Pints	100 min	**11 lb**	12 lb	13 lb	14 lb

Table 2. Recommended process time for **Fish** in a weighted-gauge pressure canner.				
			Canner Pressure (PSI) at Altitudes of	
Style of Pack	**Jar Size**	**Process Time**	**0 - 1,000 ft**	**Above 1,000 ft**
Raw	Pints	100 min	**10 lb**	15 lb

Table 3. Recommended process time for **Smoked Fish** in a dial-gauge pressure canner.

			Canner Pressure (PSI) at Altitudes of			
Style of Pack	Jar Size	Process Time	0 - 2,000 ft	2,001 - 4,000 ft	4,001 - 6,000 ft	6,001 - 8,000 ft
Raw	Pints	110 min	**11 lb**	12 lb	13 lb	14 lb

Table 4. Recommended process time for **Smoked Fish** in a weighted-gauge pressure canner.

			Canner Pressure (PSI) at Altitudes of	
Style of Pack	Jar Size	Process Time	0 - 1,000 ft	Above 1,000 ft
Raw	Pints	110 min	**10 lb**	15 lb

Dill Salmon

Yield: 4 Servings

Preparation Time: 30 Minutes (Excluding Canning Time)

Ingredients

- 2 pounds fresh salmon fillets
- 1 cup mayonnaise
- 2 tablespoons Dijon mustard
- 2 tablespoons fresh dill, chopped
- Juice of 1 lemon

Directions

1. Sterilize the jars and lids for canning.
2. Prepare the pressure canner as per the manufacturer's instructions.
3. Next, you need to cut the head and tails of the fish.
4. Then cut the fish into small pieces that fit inside your canning jars.
5. Equally, divide fish meat amongst canning jars.
6. Ensure a minimum of 1 -1/2 inch of headspace is left in each jar.
7. Stir together mayonnaise, Dijon mustard, fresh dill, and lemon juice.
8. Add the prepared dill sauce mixture over the salmon in each jar.
9. Take a plastic spatula and gently insert it into the jar along the inside edge.
10. Run it up and down between the food and the jar to release any air bubbles.
11. Wipe jars with a clean cloth.
12. Wipe the rims of the jars so they seal properly.
13. Close and tightly seal the jars.
14. Carefully place the filled jars into a pressure canner.
15. Process the canning jars in your pressure canner according to your recommended time and pressure for the altitude.
16. Next, carefully remove the jars from the canner.
17. Let the jars cool for 8-12 hours.
18. Check the seals once the jars are cooled off.
19. Clean the jars by washing them with warm, soapy water.
20. Store the labeled jars in a dry and cool place for proper preservation.

Nutrition Facts: Calories: 538 | Total Fat: 34g | Saturated Fat: 4.9g | Sodium: 610mg
Carbohydrate: 15.3g | Sugars: 3.8g | Protein: 45.2g

Easy Homemade Canned Fish

Yield: 2 Servings

Preparation Time: 30 Minutes (Excluding Canning Time)

Ingredients

- 1 pound of capelin fish
- 2.7 cups of Onion, chopped
- 4 Bay leaves
- 2.5 tablespoons Sugar
- ½ teaspoon of picking Salt (per half-pint jar)
- ½ cup Vegetable oil
- 1-1/2 tablespoons Vinegar
- 2-1/4 cups Tomato paste

Directions

1. Sterilize the jars and lids for canning.
2. Prepare the pressure canner as per the manufacturer's instructions.
3. Defrost and wash the fish thoroughly before canning.
4. Remove the head and tail of the fish and leave the fins.
5. Pour water in 1: 1 proportion into a pot and add onion, bay leaves, sugar, salt, vegetable oil, vinegar, and tomato paste; mix everything.
6. Add fish and set it on low heat for three hours, covered.
7. Put the fish together with the sauce into canning jars, leaving 1-1/2 inches of head space.
8. Take a plastic spatula and gently insert it into the jar along the inside edge.
9. Run it up and down between the food and the jar to release any air bubbles.
10. Process the jars in your pressure canner according to your recommended time and pressure.
11. Next, carefully remove the jars from the canner.
12. Let the jars cool completely.
13. Check the seals once the jars are cooled off.
14. Clean the jars by washing them with warm, soapy water. Remember to label the jars with the date and contents. Store the labeled jars in a dry and cool place for proper preservation.

Nutrition Facts: Calories: 1343 | Total Fat: 83.8g | Saturated Fat: 17.4g | Sodium: 1470mg Carbohydrate: 117.6g | Sugars: 53.5g | Protein: 46.3g

Canned Tuna in Water

Yield: 4 Servings

Preparation Time: 30 Minutes (Excluding Canning Time)

Ingredients

- 2 pounds of fresh tuna
- Water, for filling the jar
- Salt (1/2 teaspoon per pint jar)

Directions

1. Sterilize the jars and lids for canning.
2. Prepare the pressure canner as per the manufacturer's instructions.
3. First, you need to cut the tuna into sizes adjustable with jars.
4. Leave 1 1/2 inches of headspace after tightly packing the tuna into the jars.
5. For each pint jar, add 1/2 teaspoon of salt (according to taste).
6. Add water to each jar to cover the tuna and leave 1-inch headspace.
7. Take a plastic spatula and gently insert it into the jar along the inside edge.
8. Run it up and down between the food and the jar to release any air bubbles.
9. Put the lids on the jars, clean the rims, and secure the bands.
10. Process the jars in your pressure canner.
11. Refer to the table below to adjust time and pressure according to altitude.
12. Check the seals, let the jars cool, and keep them somewhere cool and dry before storing them.

Table 1. Recommended process time for **Tuna** in a dial-gauge pressure canner					
		Canner Pressure (PSI) at Altitudes of			
Jar Size	Process Time	**0 - 2,000 ft**	**2,001 - 4,000 ft**	**4,001 - 6,000 ft**	**6,001 - 8,000 ft**
Pints and Half-pints	100 min	**11 lb**	12 lb	13 lb	14 lb

Table 2. Recommended process time for **Tuna** in a weighted-gauge pressure canner.			
		Canner Pressure (PSI) at Altitudes of	
Jar Size	**Process Time**	**0 - 1,000 ft**	**Above 1,000 ft**
Pints and Half-pints	100 min	**10 lb**	15 lb

Nutrition Facts

Calories: 422 | Total Fat: 18.3g | Saturated Fat: 3.7g | Sodium: 113mg

Carbohydrate: 0g | Sugars: 0g | Protein: 60.2g

Canned Salmon

Yield: 4 Servings

Preparation Time: 30-45 Minutes (Excluding Canning Time)

Ingredients

- 2 pounds fresh salmon fillets
- ½ teaspoon pickling salt (per half-pint jar)
- Lemon juice, as needed to taste
- Pepper, to taste
- Vinegar, ½ tbsp per pint
- 2 tablespoons of fresh thyme

Directions

1. Sterilize the jars and lids for canning.
2. Prepare the pressure canner as per the manufacturer's instructions.
3. Cut the salmon fillets into bite-sized pieces to fit inside canning jars.
4. Add the salmon tightly into prepared jars, leaving 1-1/2 inch of headspace.
5. Add salt, lemon juice, pepper, vinegar, and thyme in a bowl and mix well.
6. Add this mixture over the salmon in each jar, leaving 1-inch head space.
7. Take a plastic spatula and gently insert it into the jar along the inside edge.
8. Run it up and down between the food and the jar to release any air bubbles.
9. Clean the jar rims.
10. Put the lids on the jars.
11. Tightly close the jars by securing the bands.
12. Process the jars in a pressure canner.
13. Adjust time and pressure according to altitude.
14. Next, carefully remove the jars from the canner.
15. Let the jars cool for 8-12 hours.
16. Check the seals once the jars are cooled off.
17. Remember to label the jars with the date and contents.
18. Store the labeled jars in a dry and cool place for proper preservation.

Nutrition Facts: Calories: 304 | Total Fat: 14.1g | Saturated Fat: 2g | Sodium: 341mg
Carbohydrate: 0.9g | Sugars: 0g | Protein: 44.1g

Canned Lobster Meat

Yield: 4 Servings

Preparation Time: 25 Minutes (Excluding Canning Time)

Ingredients

- 2 pounds of fresh lobster meat
- 4 cups Water
- 1/4 cup salt
- 2 tablespoons sugar

- 2 bay leaves
- 2 tablespoons of thyme, dried
- 2 tablespoon rosemary, dried
- 1 lemon, sliced

Directions

1. Sterilize the jars and lids for canning.
2. Prepare the pressure canner as per the manufacturer's instructions.
3. Leave 1-inch headspace after securely packing the lobster meat into the canning jars, leaving 1-1/2 inches head space.
4. Add 4 cups of water, salt, sugar, bay leaves, thyme, rosemary, and lemon slices in a cooking pot and combine.
5. Let it boil, and then simmer it for 8 minutes.
6. Fill the jars with this prepared water mixture, leaving 1-inch headspace.
7. Take a plastic spatula and gently insert it into the jar along the inside edge.
8. Run it up and down between the food and the jar to release any air bubbles.
9. Clean the jar rims, place the lids on the jars, and tighten the bands.
10. Process the jars in a pressure canner, and adjust time and pressure according to the altitude.
11. Take out the jars.
12. Let the jars cool, check the seal, and keep them somewhere cool and dry.

Nutrition Facts

Calories: 234 | Total Fat: 2.2g | Saturated Fat: 0.6g | Sodium: 8184mg

Carbohydrate: 7.9g | Sugars: 6g | Protein: 43.3g

Canned Shrimp

Yield: 4 Servings

Preparation Time: 15 Minutes (Excluding Canning Time)

Ingredients

- 2 pounds fresh shrimp, peeled and deveined
- Salt (1/2 teaspoon per pint jar)
- Water

Directions

1. Sterilize the jars and lids for canning.
2. Prepare the pressure canner as per the manufacturer's instructions.
3. Add the shrimp tightly into canning jars, leaving 1 -1/2 inch of headspace.
4. Add 1/2 teaspoon of salt to each pint jar
5. Fill the jars with water, leaving 1-inch headspace.
6. Take a plastic spatula and gently insert it into the jar along the inside edge.
7. Run it up and down between the food and the jar to release any air bubbles.
8. Clean the jar rims, place the lids on the jars, and tighten them to seal.
9. Process the jars in a pressure canner.
10. Adjust time and pressure according to altitude.
11. Take out the jars and let them get cool.
12. Allow the jars to cool, check the seals, and store them in a cool and dry place.

Nutrition Facts

Calories: 269 | Total Fat: 3.8g | Saturated Fat: 1.2g | Sodium: 553mg

Carbohydrate: 3.4g | Sugars: 0g | Protein: 51.7g

Canned Crab Meat

Yield: 4 Servings

Preparation Time: 15 Minutes (Excluding Canning Time)

Ingredients

- 2 pounds of fresh crab meat
- Salt (1/2 teaspoon per pint jar)
- 2 teaspoons brown sugar
- 2 tablespoons lemon juice
- 2 tablespoons of orange juice
- Water, 4 cups

Directions

1. Sterilize the jars and lids for canning.
2. Prepare the pressure canner as per the manufacturer's instructions.
3. Add the crab meat tightly into canning jars, leaving 1-1/2 inches of headspace.
4. Add 1/2 teaspoon of salt to each pint jar.
5. Then add sugar, lemon juice, and orange juice equally between each pint jar.
6. Fill the jars with water, leaving 1-inch headspace.
7. Take a plastic spatula and gently insert it into the jar along the inside edge.
8. Run it up and down between the food and the jar to release any air bubbles.
9. Clean the jar rims, place the lids on the jars, and tighten them to seal.
10. Process the jars in a pressure canner.
11. Adjust time and pressure according to altitude.
12. Take out the jars.
13. Allow the jars to cool, check the seals, and store the jars in a cool and dry place.

Nutrition Facts

Calories: 214 | Total Fat: 4.1g | Saturated Fat: 0.1g | Sodium: 1458mg
| Sugars: 2.3g | Protein: 28.5g

Table 1. Recommended process time for **King and Dungeness Crab Meat** in a dial-gauge pressure canner					
		Canner Pressure (PSI) at Altitudes of			
Jar Size	**Process Time**	**0 - 2,000 ft**	**2,001 - 4,000 ft**	**4,001 - 6,000 ft**	**6,001 - 8,000 ft**
Half-pints	70 min	**11 lb**	12 lb	13 lb	14 lb
Pints	80	**11**	12	13	14

Table 2. Recommended process time for **King and Dungeness Crab Meat** in a weighted-gauge pressure canner			
		Canner Pressure (PSI) at Altitudes of	
Jar Size	**Process Time**	**0 - 1,00 ft**	**Above 1,000 ft**
Half-pints	70 min	**10 lb**	15 lb
Pints	80	**10**	15

Canned Sardines in Tomato Sauce

Yield: 6 Servings

Preparation Time: 15-30 Minutes (Excluding Canning Time)

Ingredients

- 3 pounds fresh sardines
- 3 cups tomato sauce
- 2 teaspoons salt

- 1 teaspoon chili flakes
- 1 teaspoon of black pepper
- 2 cloves garlic, minced

Directions

1. Sterilize the jars and lids and repare the pressure canner as per the manufacturer's instructions.
2. First, thoroughly wash and clean the sardines.
3. Cut the head, scale, and guts. Rinse it under the tap water.
4. Pat it dry with a paper towel.
5. Cut the sardines into small pieces.
6. Pack the sardine pieces tightly into the jars, leaving 1-1/2 inch of headspace.
7. Press down gently.
8. Add tomato sauce, salt, chili flakes, black pepper, and minced garlic in a cooking pan.
9. Simmer it and cook it for 5 minutes.
10. Once prepared, pour this hot tomato sauce into the Jar.
11. Ensure that the sauce covers the sardines, ensuring 1-inch head space.
12. Take a plastic spatula and gently insert it into the jar along the inside edge.
13. Run it up and down between the food and the jar to release any air bubbles.
14. Clean the rims with a damp cloth.
15. Put the lids on the jars and secure them tightly.
16. Put the jars in your pressure canner according to the manufacturer's instructions.
17. Process the jars in a pressure canner.
18. Follow the recommended processing times and pressures for your specific altitude.
19. Once done, take out the jars.
20. Let the jars get cool, and then store them after inspecting the seal

Nutrition Facts: Calories: 504 | Total Fat: 26.2g | Saturated Fat: 3.5g | Sodium: 2563mg
Carbohydrate: 7.2g | Sugars: 5.2g | Protein: 57.6g

Canned Mackerel in Olive Oil

Yield: 4 Servings

Preparation Time: 15 Minutes (Excluding Canning Time)

Ingredients

- 2 pounds fresh mackerel fillets, smoked, skinless, and boneless
- 1 teaspoon salt
- 1 teaspoon paprika
- 1/2 teaspoon garlic powder
- 1/2 teaspoon of onion powder
- Olive oil, as needed

Directions

1. Wash the canning jars and sterilize those jars properly.
2. Next, prepare the pressure canner according to the manufacturer's instructions.
3. Cut the fillets into smaller pieces, about 1-inch.
4. Pack the smoked mackerel into the jars, ensuring 1-1/2 inches of headspace.
5. Add 1 teaspoon of salt, 1 teaspoon of paprika, 1/2 teaspoon of garlic powder, and ½ teaspoon of onion powder over the mackerel per jar.
6. In the end, add olive oil into each jar, covering the mackerel completely, and leave 1-inch of head space on top.
7. Take a plastic spatula and gently insert it into the jar along the inside edge.
8. Run it up and down between the food and the jar to release any air bubbles.
9. Seal the jars.
10. Process the jars in your Pressure Canner and adjust time and pressure according to your altitude.
11. Once done, remove the jars and let the jars get cool completely.
12. Check the seal.
13. Store the canning jars in a cool, dark place.

Nutrition Facts

Calories: 1030 | Total Fat: 90.9g | Saturated Fat: 16.7g | Sodium: 770mg

Carbohydrate: 0.8g | Sugars: 0.3g | Protein: 54.3g

Canned Fish in Tomato Sauce

Yield: 4 Servings

Preparation Time: 25 Minutes (Excluding Canning Time)

Ingredients

- 2 pounds salmon
- 2 tablespoons olive oil
- 1 onion, finely chopped
- 2 garlic cloves, minced
- 2 cups tomato sauce
- 1 teaspoon salt
- 1/2 teaspoon black pepper
- 1/2 teaspoon dried oregano

Directions

1. Wash the canning jars and sterilize those jars properly.
2. Next, prepare the pressure canner according to the manufacturer's instructions.
3. Cut the fish fillets into small pieces.
4. Add the olive oil into a skillet and heat over medium flame.
5. Add the onion and garlic to the skillet and sauté until translucent and fragrant.
6. Pour the tomato sauce into the skillet with the sautéed onion and garlic.
7. Stir in the salt, black pepper, and dried oregano.
8. Let the sauce simmer for 5 minutes.
9. Pack the fish fillets tightly into the jars, ensuring 1-1/2 inches of head space.
10. Next, pour the tomato sauce mixture into each jar, covering the fish completely and maintaining the 1-inch headspace.
11. Take a plastic spatula and gently insert it into the jar along the inside edge.
12. Run it up and down between the food and the jar to release any air bubbles.
13. Seal the Jars.
14. Process the Jars in your Pressure Canner at 10 pounds of pressure for 100 minutes (adjust the altitude accordingly).
15. Once done, remove the jars and let the jars get cool completely.
16. Check seal.
17. Store the canning jars in a cool, dark place.

Nutrition Facts: Calories: 404 | Total Fat: 21.3g | Saturated Fat: 3g | Sodium: 1325mg
Carbohydrate: 10g | Sugars: 6.4g | Protein: 46.1g

Beef Recipes

Guide Table For All Type Of Red Meat/Pork

Table 1. Recommended process time for **Ground or Chopped Meat** in a dial-gauge pressure canner.

			Canner Pressure (PSI) at Altitudes of			
Style of Pack	Jar Size	Process Time	0 - 2,000 ft	2,001 - 4,000 ft	4,001 - 6,000 ft	6,001 - 8,000 ft
Hot	Pints	75 min	11 lb	12 lb	13 lb	14 lb
	Quarts	90	11	12	13	14

Table 2. Recommended process time for **Ground or Chopped Meat** in a weighted-gauge pressure canner.

			Canner Pressure (PSI) at Altitudes of	
Style of Pack	Jar Size	Process Time	0 - 1,000 ft	Above 1,000 ft
Hot	Pints	75 min	10 lb	15 lb
	Quarts	90	10	15

Table 3. Recommended process time for **Strips, Cubes, or Chunks of Meat** in a dial-gauge pressure canner.

Style of Pack	Jar Size	Process Time	Canner Pressure (PSI) at Altitudes of			
			0 - 2,000 ft	2,001 - 4,000 ft	4,001 - 6,000 ft	6,001 - 8,000 ft
Hot and Raw	Pints	75 min	**11 lb**	12 lb	13 lb	14 lb
	Quarts	90	**11**	12	13	14

Table 4. Recommended process time for **Strips, Cubes, or Chunks of Meat** in a weighted-gauge pressure canner.

Style of Pack	Jar Size	Process Time	Canner Pressure (PSI) at Altitudes of	
			0 - 1,000 ft	Above 1,000 ft
Hot and Raw	Pints	75 min	**10 lb**	15 lb
	Quarts	90	**10**	15

Note: approximately 1/2 to 1 cup of beef broth/water per quart-sized (32-ounce) jar of canned meat is needed.

Pressure Canned Sausage

Yield: 4 Servings

Preparation Time: 15-25 Minutes (Excluding Canning Time)

Ingredients

- 2 pounds sausage, cubed 1-inches
- 2 teaspoons of olive oil
- Tomato juice to fill the jars

Directions

1. Sterilize the jars and lids for canning.
2. Prepare the pressure canner as per the manufacturer's instructions.
3. Cut link sausages into 3 to 10 cm (1 to 4-inch) pieces.
4. Lightly brown in a frying pan using olive oil.
5. Drain excess fat.
6. Pack hot sausages into preheated ½ liter (US pint) or 1 liter (US quart) jars.
7. Leave 1-1/2 inches of headspace.
8. Take a plastic spatula and gently insert it into the jar along the inside edge.
9. Run it up and down between the food and the jar to release any air bubbles.
10. Fill jars with tomato juice, leaving 1-inch of headspace.
11. Remove air bubbles and adjust the headspace.
12. Wipe jar rims.
13. Apply lids.
14. Process cans in a pressure canner.
15. Adjust time and pressure settings according to altitude.
16. Take out the jars and let the jars cool.
17. Check the seal.
18. Store in a cool and dry place.

Nutrition Facts

Calories: 789 | Total Fat: 66.7g | Saturated Fat: 21g | Sodium: 1699mg

Carbohydrate: 0g | Sugars: 0g | Protein: 44.1g

Pressure Canned Beef Chunks

Yield: 25-28 Servings

Preparation Time: 35-60 Minutes (Excluding Canning Time)

Ingredients

- 13 pounds beef cut about 1-inch
- 3 heads garlic, crushed
- 4 teaspoons of onion powder
- 9 teaspoons of sea salt
- 4 teaspoons of black pepper
- 1-3/4 cup palm fruit shortening (divided 1/4 cup portions)

Directions

1. Sterilize the jars and lids for canning.
2. Prepare the pressure canner as per the manufacturer's instructions.
3. Rub the meat with garlic, onion powder, salt, and pepper.
4. Pack the meat into jars and push down, ensuring 1-1/2 inches headspace.
5. Add palm fruit shortening on top of each jar, ensuring 1-inch headspace.
6. Use a wooden spoon to remove air bubbles and compact the meat.
7. Seal the jars tightly.
8. Place the jars inside and process at 10 pounds of pressure for 90 minutes or adjust the time and pressure according to your altitude.
9. Once done, remove the jars and let them cool.
10. Check the seal of the jars.
11. Store it in a dark, cool place.

Nutrition Facts

Calories: 423 | Total Fat: 14.1g | Saturated Fat: 5.3g | Sodium: 797mg

Carbohydrate: 0.5g | Sugars: 0.1g | Protein: 68.9g

Beef Chunk

Yield: 10 Servings

Preparation Time: 35-60 Minutes (Excluding Canning Time)

Ingredients

- 5 pounds of beef chunks, cubed into 1-inch
- 5 cups beef broth
- 1 tablespoon salt
- 1 tablespoon of pepper
- 1 tablespoon of onion powder
- 1 tablespoon of thyme

Directions

1. Wash the canning jars and sterilized jars properly.
2. Put them in a pot of hot water to keep them warm.
3. Prepare your pressure canner.
4. Remove excess fat from meat.
5. Bring the broth to a simmering boil in a large cooking pot.
6. Add the beef pieces to the boiling broth and simmer for 2-3 minutes.
7. Transfer the beef pieces to each jar, leaving 1-1/2 inches headspace.
8. Add salt, pepper, onion powder, and thyme to each jar.
9. Pour the hot broth into the jars, leaving 1-inch headspace.
10. Remove any air bubbles and place the jars in the pressure canner according to the manufacturer's instructions, ensuring proper placement and water level.
11. Close and lock the canner lid, making sure the vent is closed.
12. Adjust the time and pressure according to your altitude.
13. Use a jar lifter to move the jars onto a countertop lined with a towel.
14. Let them cool undisturbed for 24 hours.
15. To check the seals, press the center of each lid.
16. The jar is properly sealed if it feels firm and doesn't flex.
17. If jars don't seal, refrigerate and consume them within a few days.

Nutrition Facts: Calories: 267 | Total Fat: 8.8g | Saturated Fat: 4.3g | Sodium: 3915mg Carbohydrate: 5.7g | Sugars: 0.6g | Protein: 39g

Chili Con Carne

Yield: 6 Servings

Preparation Time: 45-60 Minutes (Excluding Canning Time)

Ingredients

- 3 pounds of pinto beans, soaked overnight, then drained and rinsed
- 3 tablespoons vegetable oil
- 3 pounds lean ground beef
- 4 large yellow onions, chopped
- 8 cloves garlic, minced
- ⅓ Cup chili powder
- 2 tablespoons sugar
- 2 tablespoons salt
- 2-3 tablespoons ground cumin
- 2 tablespoons beef bouillon granules/powder
- 1 teaspoon black pepper
- 1 tablespoon onion powder
- 2 teaspoons garlic powder
- 6 (14.5 ounces) cans of diced tomatoes
- 6 (14.5 ounces) cans of tomato sauce
- 3 cups water

Directions

1. Wash the canning jars and sterilized jars properly.
2. Put them in a pot of hot water to keep them warm.
3. Prepare your pressure canner.
4. Place soaked and rinsed beans in clean water in a Dutch oven and bring to s rapid boil.
5. Reduce the heat and simmer it for 30 minutes.
6. Drain and rinse. Set aside.
7. Heat oil in a clean Dutch oven over medium heat
8. Add the beef and cook until brown.
9. Next, add the onions and garlic and cook until soft and translucent.
10. Add seasonings and cook for an additional minute.
11. Add all remaining ingredients, boil, reduce heat, and simmer for 5 minutes.
12. Ladle chili into hot sterilized jars, leaving 1-inch of headspace.
13. Tap jars to remove any air bubbles.
14. Place lids on each jar and screw on the rims firmly but not excessively.
15. Follow the instructions for processing in your pressure canner.

16. Remove jars and let them sit undisturbed for 24 hours; check the seal, then store them in a cool, dark place.

Nutrition Facts

Calories: 1539 | Total Fat: 27g | Saturated Fat: 7.6g | Sodium: 4759mg

Carbohydrate: 201.1g | Sugars: 42.5g | Protein: 129.3g

Sloppy Joe Mix With Meat

Yield: 12 Servings

Preparation Time: 35-40 Minutes (Excluding Canning Time)

Ingredients

- 6 pounds of ground beef
- 4 cups of tomato sauce
- 2 cups beef broth
- 2 cups of whet onion, finely diced
- 1 cup green bell pepper, finely diced
- 7 cloves garlic, minced

- 1/4 cup maple syrup or honey
- 1/4 cup apple cider vinegar
- 6 teaspoons Worcestershire sauce
- 2 teaspoons yellow mustard
- 1/2 teaspoon salt
- 1/2 teaspoon ground black pepper

Directions

1. Wash the canning jars and sterilized jars properly.
2. Take a Dutch oven and brown beef in it.
3. You can work in batches to cook meat.
4. Remove any excess fat.
5. Combine the remaining ingredients in the Dutch oven and bring it to a boil.
6. Boil the mixture vigorously for 10 minutes, stirring frequently to prevent scorching.
7. Use a spoon to transfer the hot mixture into hot canning jars, leaving 1-inch of headspace.
8. Remove any air bubbles and adjust to maintain the headspace.
9. Wipe the rims of the jars.
10. Tightly close the jars.
11. Put the jars in your pressure canner.
12. Follow the instructions for processing in your pressure canner according to your altitude.
13. Remove jars and let them sit undisturbed for 24 hours; check the seal, then store them in a cool, dark place.

Nutrition Facts

Calories: 475 | Total Fat: 14.6g | Saturated Fat: 5.4g | Sodium: 840mg

Carbohydrate: 10.9g | Sugars: 8.5g | Protein: 71g

Canned Beef Chili

Yield: 10 Servings

Preparation Time: 35-40 Minutes (Excluding Canning Time)

Ingredients

- 5 pounds of ground beef
- 4 cups diced tomatoes
- 2 cups kidney beans
- 2 cups chopped onions
- 4 teaspoons chili powder
- 1 tablespoon salt (optional)

Directions

1. Wash the canning jars and sterilized jars properly.
2. Put them in a pot of hot water to keep them warm.
3. Prepare your pressure canner.
4. Take a skillet and brown the ground beef in it.
5. Drain any excess fat.
6. Combine the cooked ground beef, tomatoes, kidney beans, onions, chili powder, and salt in a large pot.
7. Simmer it for 10 minutes.
8. Transfer the chili to clean, sterilized canning jars.
9. Remove air bubbles and adjust the headspace.
10. Clean the jar rims, then position the lids and bands on the jars.
11. Tighten them with your fingertips until snug.
12. Put the jars in a pressure canner and process them at the recommended pressure and processing time for ground beef (typically 75 minutes for pints or 90 minutes for quarts).
13. Adjust according to altitude.
14. Take it out, and let it get cool.
15. Check the seal.
16. Store jars in a cool dark place.

Nutrition Facts

Calories: 571 | Total Fat: 14.9g | Saturated Fat: 5.4g | Sodium: 866mg

Carbohydrate: 28.1g | Sugars: 3.7g | Protein: 78.1g

Meat In Spaghetti Sauce

Yield: 10 Servings

Preparation Time: 40 Minutes (Excluding Canning Time)

Ingredients

- 5 pounds of ground beef
- 10 cups tomato sauce
- 2 cups onions, chopped

- 2 cups green bell peppers, chopped
- 4 cloves garlic, minced
- 2 teaspoons salt

Directions

1. Wash the canning jars and sterilize them properly.
2. Put them in a pot of hot water to keep them warm.
3. Prepare your pressure canner.
4. Take a skillet and brown beef over medium heat.
5. Drain any excess fat.
6. Add tomato sauce, onions, green bell peppers, minced garlic, and salt in a skillet.
7. Simmer for 15 minutes.
8. Transfer the meat sauce into sterilized canning jars, leaving 1-inch headspace.
9. Remove air bubbles and adjust the headspace.
10. Clean the jar rims, position the lids and bands on the jars, and tighten them with your fingertips until snug.
11. Add the jars into a pressure canner and process them at the recommended pressure and processing time for ground beef according to your specific altitude, typically 75 minutes for pints or 90 minutes for quarts.
12. Take it out, and let it get cool.
13. Check the seal and then store it.

Nutrition Facts

Calories: 499 | Total Fat: 14.7g | Saturated Fat: 5.4g | Sodium: 1900mg
Carbohydrate: 17.5g | Sugars: 12.6g | Protein: 72.6g

Beef Chuck In Sauce

Yield: 6-10 Servings

Preparation Time: 25-30 Minutes (Excluding Canning Time)

Ingredients

- 2 tablespoons olive oil
- 5 pounds of beef chuck, cut into 1-inch cubes
- 2 cups diced tomatoes
- 1 cup tomato paste
- 4 cups beef broth
- 1 cup chopped onions
- 4 cloves garlic, minced
- 2 teaspoons salt
- 2 teaspoons black pepper

Directions

1. Wash the canning jars and sterilized jars properly.
2. Put them in a pot of hot water to keep them warm.
3. Prepare your pressure canner.
4. Take a skillet and heat olive oil over medium heat.
5. Add the beef.
6. Simmer the beef until brown.
7. Then add tomatoes and tomato paste, and cook for 2 minutes.
8. Add beef broth, onions, garlic, salt, and black pepper, and stir well.
9. Cook for 8 minutes.
10. Transfer the beef and sauce to clean, sterilized canning jars, leaving 1-inch headspace.
11. Remove air bubbles from the jars.
12. Wipe the jar rims, place the lids and bands, and tighten them fingertip-tight.
13. Process the jars in your pressure canner at the recommended pressure and processing time for beef chuck according to altitude.
14. Remove jars, check the seal, and let it get cool.
15. Store in a dark place.

Nutrition Facts

Calories: 1539 | Total Fat: 27g | Saturated Fat: 7.6g | Sodium: 4759mg

Carbohydrate: 201.1g | Sugars: 42.5g | Protein: 129.3g

Classic Pressure Canned Grinds Beef

Yield: 10 Servings

Preparation Time: 20 Minutes (Excluding Canning Time)

Ingredients

- 5 pounds of ground beef
- 2 teaspoons salt

Directions

1. Wash the canning jars and sterilize them properly.
2. Next, prepare the pressure canner according to the manufacturer's instructions.
3. Take a large skillet and brown beef over medium heat.
4. Drain any excess fat.
5. Next, sterilize the canning jars.
6. Add the cooked ground beef into clean, sterilized canning jars, ensuring a 1-inch headspace.
7. Put about 1/4 teaspoon of salt in each pint-sized jar or 1/2 teaspoon in each quart-sized jar.
8. Remove air bubbles from the jars.
9. Wipe the jar rims, place the lids and bands, and tighten them fingertip-tight.
10. Process the jars in your pressure canner at the recommended pressure and processing time for beef chuck (usually 75 minutes for pints or 90 minutes for quarts).
11. Remove jars, check the seal, and let it get cool.
12. Store it in a cool dark place.

Nutrition Facts

Calories: 421 | Total Fat: 14.1g | Saturated Fat: 5.3g | Sodium: 614mg

Carbohydrate: 0g | Sugars: 0g | Protein: 68.8g

Beef Stroganoff

Yield: 10 Servings

Preparation Time: 30 Minutes (Excluding Canning Time)

Ingredients

- 1 teaspoon black pepper, ground
- 2 teaspoons salt
- 2 teaspoons thyme dried
- 2 teaspoons parsley dried
- 2 tablespoons of rosemary, dried
- 4 tablespoons tomato paste
- 2 cloves garlic, minced
- 4 tablespoons Worcestershire sauce
- 1 cup mushrooms, sliced
- 1 cup onion, chopped
- 2 pounds of beef chuck
- Beef broth (hot), for filing up the jars

Directions

13. Wash the canning jars and sterilize them properly.
14. Next, prepare the pressure canner according to the manufacturer's instructions.
15. Take a mixing bowl and add the listed ingredients till onion.
    Trim the fat from the beef and add it to the bowl; mix well.
16. Pack the hot jars firmly with the meat mixture.
17. Leave about 1-1/2 inches headspace.
18. Top the jars with hot beef broth.
19. Remove air bubbles.
20. Adjust 1-inch headspace and clean jar rims.
21. Put lids on top and seal the jar.
22. Process the jars in your pressure canner at the recommended pressure and processing time for beef chuck.
23. Remove jars, check the seal, and let it get cool.
24. Store it in a cool dark place.

Nutrition Facts

Calories: 199 | Total Fat: 6.2g | Saturated Fat: 2.3g | Sodium: 787mg

Carbohydrate: 4.7g | Sugars: 2.8g | Protein: 29.4g

Basic Round Steak

Yield: 10 Servings

Preparation Time: 30 Minutes (Excluding Canning Time)

Ingredients

- 5 pounds of round steak
- Salt, to taste
- Water to fill the jars

Directions

1. Sterilized the canning jars and prepare the pressure canner according to the manufacturer's instructions.
2. Remove any fat from the meat.
3. Next, rub the steak with salt.
4. Take a skillet and brown the steak on both sides.
5. Next, transfer it to a clean cutting board and let it cool completely.
6. Cut the steak into about 1-inch pieces.
7. Pack the steak tightly into sterilized canning jars, leaving about 1-1/2 inches of headspace.
8. Next, pour boiling water over the meat, ensuring the steak is fully covered, leaving 1-inch headspace.
9. Remove the air bubbles.
10. Wipe the jar rims with a clean and damp kitchen towel.
11. Put lids on top and seal the jar.
12. Close the canner lid and bring it to the recommended pressure for your altitude.
13. Process the jars at the specified pressure and time for round steak.
14. Remove jars, let them get cool, check the seal, and let it get cool.
15. Store in a cool dark place

Nutrition Facts

Calories: 490 | Total Fat: 21.8g | Saturated Fat: 8.2g | Sodium: 152mg
Carbohydrate: 0g | Sugars: 0g | Protein: 68.4g

Seasoned Round Steak

Yield: 10 Servings

Preparation Time: 30 Minutes (Excluding Canning Time)

Ingredients

- 5 pounds of round steak
- Salt (optional)
- 1 tablespoon of black pepper
- 1 tablespoon of garlic powder
- 1 tablespoon of onion powder
- Beef broth to fill the jars

Directions

1. Sterilized the canning jars and prepare the pressure canner according to the manufacturer's instructions.
2. Remove any fat from the meat.
3. Next, rub the steak with salt, black pepper, garlic powder, and onion powder.
4. Take a skillet and brown the steak.
5. Next, transfer the meat to a tray and let it cool completely.
6. Cut the steak into smaller pieces so it is inside jars.
7. Pack the steak tightly into sterilized canning jars, leaving about 1-1/2 inches of headspace.
8. Next, pour boiling water over the meat, ensuring the steak is fully covered, leaving 1-inch headspace.
9. Remove the air bubbles.
10. Wipe the jar rims with a clean and damp kitchen towel.
11. Put lids on top and seal the jar.
12. Close the canner lid and bring it to the recommended pressure for your altitude.
13. Process the jars at the specified pressure and time for round steak.
14. Remove jars, let them get cool, check the seal, and let it get cool.
15. Store in a cool dark place

Nutrition Facts

Calories: 451 | Total Fat: 11.3g | Saturated Fat: 3.9g | Sodium: 102mg

Carbohydrate: 0g | Sugars: 0g | Protein: 81.9g

Raw Pack Beef

Yield: 10 Servings

Preparation Time: 10 Minutes (Excluding Canning Time)

Ingredients

- 5 pounds of beef chunks, cubed into 1-inch pieces
- Salt (optional)

Directions

1. Sterilized the canning jars and prepare the pressure canner according to the manufacturer's instructions.
2. Remove any fat from the meat.
3. Next, rub the steak with salt.
4. Pack the raw beef tightly into sterilized canning jars, leaving t 1-inch of headspace.
5. Remove the air bubbles from the jar.
6. Wipe jar rims, and seal with lids and rings.
7. Process jars in a pressure canner according to the recommended pressure for your altitude.
8. Depressurize the canner, remove the jars, and let them cool for 12 hours.
9. Check lids for a proper seal.
10. Store it in a cool, dark place.

Nutrition Facts

Calories: 243 | Total Fat: 8.1g | Saturated Fat: 4.1g | Sodium: 2835mg

Carbohydrate: 4.1g | Sugars: 0g | Protein: 36.5g

Pressure Canned Bolognaise

Yield: 10 Servings

Preparation Time: 30 Minutes (Excluding Canning Time)

Ingredients

- 2 tablespoons vegetable oil
- 2 cups white onion, diced
- 2 tablespoons garlic, minced
- 2/3 cup tomato paste
- 2.2 pounds of ground beef
- 2 x 800 grams diced tomatoes, store-brought
- 3 cups water, filtered
- 2 cups carrot, diced
- 2 cups celery, diced
- 2 tablespoons dried oregano
- Salt and black pepper, to taste

Directions

1. Sterilized the canning jars
2. Prepare the pressure canner according to the manufacturer's instructions.
3. Take a skillet and heat the oil over medium heat.
4. Then add onions and garlic and sauté for a few minutes.
5. Now add the tomato paste in and cook for 1 minute.
6. Next, put the beef meat and cook until it gets brown.
7. Now put tomatoes and water.
8. Mix everything well.
9. Add carrots, celery, and oregano and let it boil.
10. Simmer for 60 minutes, covered
11. Add salt and pepper at this stage.
12. Prepare the canning jars.
13. Pour the prepared hot Bolognese with the help of a spoon into the hot jars, leaving 1-inch headspace.
14. Remove air bubbles from the jars.
15. Wipe jar rims, and seal with lids and rings.
16. Process jars in a pressure canner according to the recommended pressure for your altitude.
17. Depressurize the canner, remove the jars, and let them cool for 12 hours.

18. Check lids for a proper seal.

19. Store it in a cool, dark place.

Nutrition Facts

Calories: 250 | Total Fat: 9.2g | Saturated Fat: 2.9g | Sodium: 118mg

Carbohydrate: 9.4g | Sugars: 4.5g | Protein: 31.8g

Pressure Canned Greek-Style Meat

Yield: 10 Servings

Preparation Time: 35 Minutes (Excluding Canning Time)

Ingredients

- 5 pounds of beef, cut into small pieces
- Salt and pepper (to taste)
- 1 onion, chopped
- 4 cloves of garlic, minced
- 14.5 ounces diced tomatoes
- 1/2 cup of tomato paste
- ¼ cup of red wine vinegar
- 1 tablespoon of oregano, dried
- 1 teaspoon of basil, dried
- 1 teaspoon of thyme, dried
- Teaspoon rosemary, dried
- 1 teaspoon of paprika
- 1 teaspoon of cinnamon
- Water, as needed

Directions

1. Sterilize the canning jars and prepare the pressure canner according to the manufacturer's instructions.
2. Rub the meat with salt and black pepper according to the taste
3. Take a skillet and brown the meat over medium-high; set it aside.
4. In the same skillet, sauté the onion and garlic until the aroma comes.
5. Put in the tomatoes, tomato paste, red wine vinegar, dried oregano, dried basil, dried thyme, rosemary, paprika, and cinnamon.
6. Mix everything well.
7. Return the browned meat to the skillet and stir it together with spices.
8. Pour enough water so the meat is well covered.
9. Let the meat simmer for 10 minutes, allowing the flavors to melt together.
10. Pack the meat tightly into sterilized canning jars, leaving 1-inch of headspace.
11. Remove air bubbles from the jars.
12. Wipe jar rims, and seal with lids and rings.
13. Process jars in a pressure canner according to recommended time and pressure for your altitude.
14. Depressurize the canner, remove the jars, and let them cool for 12 hours.
15. Check lids for a proper seal.
16. Store it in a cool, dark place.

Nutrition Facts: Calories: 450 | Total Fat: 14.4g | Saturated Fat: 5.4g | Sodium: 165mg

Carbohydrate: 6.3g | Sugars: 3.2g | Protein: 70g

Pressure Canned Sausage in Beef Broth

Yield: 4 Servings

Preparation Time: 20 Minutes (Excluding Canning Time)

Ingredients

- 2 pounds sausage, beef sausages, 1-inch cubes
- 2 teaspoons of olive oil
- Beef broth to fill the jars

Directions

1. Sterilize the canning jars and prepare the pressure canner according to the manufacturer's instructions.
2. Cut link sausages into 1-inch pieces.
3. In a pan, brown the sausages at medium heat.
4. Drain excess fat.
5. Pack hot sausages into preheated ½ liter (US pint) or 1 liter (US quart) jars.
6. Leave -1/2 inches of headspace.
7. Fill jars with beef broth, leaving 1-inch of headspace.
8. Remove air bubbles and adjust the headspace.
9. Wipe jar rims.
10. Apply lids.
11. Process the jars at the specified pressure and time for sausages (usually around 75-90 minutes at 10 pounds of pressure.
12. Depressurize the canner, remove the jars, and let them cool for 12 hours.
13. Check lids for a proper seal.
14. Store it in a cool, dark place.

Nutrition Facts

Calories: 631 | Total Fat: 53.3g | Saturated Fat: 16.8g | Sodium: 1359mg

Carbohydrate: 0g | Sugars: 0g | Protein: 35.3g

Sausages With Herbs And Spices

Yield: 5 servings

Preparation Time: 20 Minutes (Excluding Canning Time)

Ingredients

- 2 pounds of Italian sausages, cubed into 1-inch
- Salt and pepper, to taste
- 1 onion, chopped
- 4 cloves of garlic, minced
- 14.5 ounces of diced tomatoes
- 6 ounces of tomato paste
- 1 teaspoon of oregano, dried
- 1 teaspoon of basil, dried
- 1/2 teaspoon of thyme, dried
- 1/2 teaspoon of sugar (optional)
- Water, to taste

Directions

1. Sterilize the canning jars
2. Prepare the pressure canner according to the manufacturer's instructions.
3. Cook the sausages over medium heat in a skillet until browned.
4. Season the sausages with salt and black pepper.
5. Set the sausages aside to cool.
6. In the same skillet, cook the onion with garlic until the aroma comes.
7. Put the diced tomatoes, tomato paste, oregano, basil, thyme, and sugar and stir well.
8. Return the sausages to the skillet and mix it with tomato sauce.
9. Add water so it covers the sausages fully.
10. Simmer for 10 minutes.
11. Pack the sausages and tomato sauce tightly into sterilized canning jars, leaving 1-inch headspace.
12. Remove air bubbles and adjust the headspace.
13. Wipe jar rims.
14. Apply lids.
15. Process the jars at the specified pressure and time for sausages (usually around 75-90 minutes at 10 pounds of pressure.
16. Depressurize the canner, remove the jars, and let them cool for 12 hours.
17. Check lids for a proper seal.
18. Store in a cool, dark place.

Nutrition Facts: Calories: 686 | Total Fat: 57.2g | Saturated Fat: 20.5g | Sodium: 1365mg

Carbohydrate: 14.3g | Sugars: 7.7g | Protein: 28.5g

Savory Beef With Vegetables

Yield: 10 Servings

Preparation Time: 45 Minutes (Excluding Canning Time)

Ingredients

- 5 pounds of beef stew meat, cubed
- Salt and black pepper, to taste
- 2 small white onions, chopped
- 6 cloves of garlic, minced
- 3 carrots, peeled and sliced
- 3 potatoes, peeled and diced
- 2 cups of green beans, trimmed and cut into bite-sized pieces
- 4 cups of beef broth
- 3 teaspoons of dried thyme
- 3 teaspoons of dried rosemary
- 2 bay leaves
- Water, as needed

Directions

1. Sterilize the canning jars
2. Prepare the pressure canner according to the manufacturer's instructions.
3. Season the stew meat with salt and black pepper according to taste.
4. Take a skillet and brown the beef stew meat over medium-high heat.
5. Remove the meat from the skillet and set it aside.
6. In the same skillet, sauté the onions and garlic until aroma comes.
7. Add the carrots, potatoes, and green beans to the skillet, and stir well.
8. Return the browned beef stew meat to the skillet, and mix well.
9. Add the beef broth, dried thyme, rosemary, and bay leaves to the meat.
10. Add enough water to the skillet to fully cover the ingredients.
11. Simmer and cook it for about 5-10 minutes.
12. Pack the savory beef and vegetable mixture tightly into sterilized canning jars, leaving 1-inch headspace.
13. Remove air bubbles and adjust the headspace.
14. Wipe jar rims.
15. Apply lids.

16. Process the jars at the specified pressure and time for meat and vegetables (usually around 90 minutes at 10 pounds of pressure).

17. Depressurize the canner, remove the jars, and let them cool for 12 hours.

18. Check lids for a proper seal.

19. Store in a cool, dark place.

Nutrition Facts

Calories: 505 | Total Fat: 14.9g | Saturated Fat: 5.6g | Sodium: 474mg
Carbohydrate: 16.1g | Sugars: 2.8g | Protein: 72.7g

Beef With Indian Spices

Yield: 10 Servings

Preparation Time: 45 Minutes (Excluding Canning Time)

Ingredients

- 5 pounds of beef stew meat, cubed
- Salt and black pepper, to taste
- 2 tablespoons vegetable oil
- 4 cloves of garlic, minced
- 2 onions, chopped
- 1 tablespoon ground cumin
- 1 tablespoon ground coriander
- 1 tablespoon ground turmeric
- ½ tablespoon ground cinnamon
- ½ tablespoon ground ginger
- 1 tablespoon chili powder
- 14 ounces of diced tomatoes
- 2 cups beef broth
- Water, as needed

Directions

1. Seasoning the beef stew meat with salt and pepper according to taste.
2. Take a pressure cooker or pot and heat the oil over medium-high heat.
3. Brown the beef stew meat in small batches, brown both sides, and set aside.
4. Add the minced garlic and onion to the same pot. Sauté onions until transparent and fragrant.
5. Add the ground cumin, coriander, cinnamon, ginger, chili powder, onions, and garlic to the pot. Combine well.
6. Re-add the beef stew meat browned to the pot, then combine it with the spicy onion mixture.
7. Next, add the diced tomatoes and beef broth. Stir to mix.
8. Add more water as necessary to ensure the meat and veggies are completely covered in liquid.
9. Simmer the mixture for a short while. If cooking beef stew in a pressure cooker, cover the container and follow the manufacturer's directions (typically, 45 minutes under pressure). If using a standard saucepan, covers it and cook the meat for two to three hours or until it is soft.
10. Let the mixture cool when the beef is cooked and tender.
11. Fill sterilized canning jars with the chilled beef and sauce, leaving 1-inch of headspace.
12. Wipe jar rims.
13. Remove bubbles.
14. Apply lids.

15. Process the jars at the specified pressure and time for meat.

16. Depressurize the canner, remove the jars, and let them cool for 12 hours.

17. Check lids for a proper seal.

18. Store it in a cool, dark place.

Nutrition Facts

Calories: 480 | Total Fat: 17.6g | Saturated Fat: 6g | Sodium: 314mg

Carbohydrate: 5.8g | Sugars: 2.2g | Protein: 70.7g

Sage and Cayenne spiced Round Steak

Yield: 10 Servings

Preparation Time: 20-30 Minutes (Excluding Canning Time)

Ingredients

- 5 pounds of round steak
- Salt (optional)
- 1 tablespoon of black pepper
- 1 tablespoon of sage
- 1 tablespoon of cayenne pepper
- Beef broth to fill the jars

Directions

1. Sterilized the canning jars and prepare the pressure canner according to the
2. Remove any fat from the meat.
3. Next, rub the steak with salt, black pepper, sage, and cayenne.
4. Take a skillet and brown the steak on each side.
5. Next, transfer the steak to a cutting board and let it cool completely.
6. Cut his steak into small pieces to fit in the jars.
7. Pack the steak tightly into sterilized canning jars, leaving about 1-inch headspace.
8. Next, pour boiling water over the meat, ensuring the steak is fully covered, leaving 1-inch headspace.
9. Remove the air bubbles.
10. Wipe the jar rims with a clean and damp kitchen towel.
11. Put lids on top and seal the jar.
12. Close the canner lid and bring it to the recommended pressure for your altitude.
13. Process the jars at the specified pressure and time for round steak.
14. Remove jars, let them get cool, check the seal, and let it get cool.
15. Store in a cool, dark place

Nutrition Facts

Calories: 494 | Total Fat: 22g | Saturated Fat: 8.3g | Sodium: 152mg

Carbohydrate: 0.8g | Sugars: 0.1g | Protein: 68.6g

Canned Beef in Tomato Juice

Yield: 10 Servings

Preparation Time: 10-15 Minutes (Excluding Canning Time)

Ingredients

- 5 pounds of beef stew meat, cubed about 1-inch pieces
- Salt and black pepper, to taste
- Tomato juice to cover the beef

Directions

1. Sterilize the canning jars and prepare the pressure canner according to the manufacturer's instructions.
2. Remove any fat from the meat.
3. Rub the beef stew meat with salt and black pepper according to taste.
4. Pack the seasoned beef tightly into sterilized canning jars, and ensure 1-inch headspace at the top.
5. Add beef to each canning jar.
6. Pour enough tomato juice to fill each jar.
7. Ensure that the tomato juice fills all the spaces between the meats.
8. Remove any air bubbles.
9. Put lids on top and seal the jar.
10. Close the canner lid and bring it to the recommended pressure and time for your altitude.
11. Remove jars, let them get cool, check the seal, and let it get cool.
12. Store in a cool, dark place.

Nutrition Facts

Calories: 421 | Total Fat: 14.1g | Saturated Fat: 5.3g | Sodium: 149mg

Carbohydrate: 0g | Sugars: 0g | Protein: 68.8g

Sweet Beef

Yield: 10 Servings

Preparation Time: 20 Minutes (Excluding Canning Time)

Ingredients

- 5 pounds beef chuck roast, cut into pieces about 1-inch
- Salt and black pepper, to taste
- 1 cup brown sugar
- 1/2 cup soy sauce
- 1/2 cup ketchup
- 1/4 cup apple cider vinegar
- 2 tablespoons Worcestershire sauce
- 4 cloves garlic, minced
- 1 teaspoon ground ginger
- Water, as needed

Directions

1. Sterilize the canning jars and prepare the pressure canner according to the manufacturer's instructions.
2. Season the beef roast pieces with salt and black pepper according to taste.
3. Combine brown sugar, soy sauce, ketchup, apple cider vinegar, Worcestershire sauce, minced garlic, and ground ginger in a large bowl. Mix it well.
4. Place the seasoned beef pieces into a large pot.
5. Pour the prepared sauce mixture over the beef, ensuring all the pieces are coated.
6. Pour the water into the pot to ensure the beef is fully covered, and stir it well.
7. Cover the pot and cook meat for 3 hours.
8. The meat should be tender till now
9. Let the meat get cool.
10. Transfer the cooled sweet beef and sauce into sterilized canning jars, leaving 1-inch of headspace.
11. Remove any air bubbles by running a utensil or bubble remover tool along the inside edges of the jar.
12. Put lids on top and seal the jar.
13. Close the canner lid and bring it to the recommended pressure for your altitude.
14. Process the jars at the specified pressure and time according to recommended guidelines for canning beef.
15. Remove jars, let them get cool, check the seal, and let it get cool.

16. Store in a cool, dark place.

Nutrition Facts

Calories: 903 | Total Fat: 63.2g | Saturated Fat: 25.1g | Sodium: 1035mg

Carbohydrate: 19.4g | Sugars: 17.7g | Protein: 60.5g

Beef With Corn

Yield: 4 Servings

Preparation Time: 10 Minutes (Excluding Canning Time)

Ingredients

- 4 cups fresh corn kernels
- 2 cups cooked beef (stew meat or shredded beef)
- Salt (optional)
- Beef broth

Directions

1. Sterilized the canning jars and prepare the pressure canner according to the manufacturer's instructions.
2. Remove any fat from the meat.
3. Blanch fresh corn kernels by boiling them for a few minutes.
4. Next, transfer corn kernels to a bowl filled with cold water.
5. Layer 1 cup of blanched corn kernels and 1/2 cup of cooked beef and salt as needed to sterilized jars, leaving 1-inch headspace
6. Fill jars with beef broth, covering the corn and beef and ensuring 1-inch headspace.
7. Remove any air bubbles by running a utensil or bubble remover tool along the inside edges of the jar.
8. Clean the jars.
9. Put lids on top and seal the jar.
10. Close the canner lid and bring it to the recommended pressure for your altitude.
11. Process the jars at the specified pressure and time according to recommended guidelines for canning beef.
12. Remove jars, let them get cool completely, check the seal, and let them get cool.
13. Store it in a cool, dark place.

Nutrition Facts

Calories: 630 | Total Fat: 18.6g | Saturated Fat: 6.5g | Sodium: 701mg

Carbohydrate: 29.6g | Sugars: 5.4g | Protein: 85.4g

Five Spice Canned Beef

Yield: 10 Servings

Preparation Time: 10-20 Minutes (Excluding Canning Time)

Ingredients

- 5 pounds of beef roast, cut into pieces
- Salt and black pepper, to taste
- 1 tablespoon Chinese five-spice powder
- 4 teaspoons soy sauce
- 4 teaspoons brown sugar
- 4 cups beef broth

Directions

1. Season the meat pieces with salt and black pepper.
2. Mix the Chinese five-spice powder, soy sauce, and brown sugar in a bowl.
3. Place the beef pieces in a Ziploc bag, and pour the marinade. Shake it well, and let it sit in the refrigerator for 24 hours.
4. Preheat your pressure canner according to the manufacturer's instructions.
5. Remove the beef from the bag and place them in sterilized canning jars, leaving about 1-inch of headspace.
6. Pour the beef broth into sterilized canning jars, leaving 1-inch of headspace.
7. Remove any air bubbles.
8. Clean the jars.
9. Put lids on top and seal the jar.
10. Close the canner lid and bring it to the recommended pressure for your altitude.
11. Process the jars at the specified pressure and time according to recommended guidelines for canning beef.
12. Remove jars, let them get cool completely, check the seal, and let it get cool.
13. Store it in a cool, dark place.

Nutrition Facts

Calories: 442 | Total Fat: 14.7g | Saturated Fat: 5.5g | Sodium: 574mg

Carbohydrate: 1.7g | Sugars: 1.5g | Protein: 70.9g

Beef Roast With Hoisin Sauce

Yield: 10 Servings

Preparation Time: 45-60 Minutes (Excluding Canning Time)

Ingredients

- 5 pounds of beef roast, cut into pieces
- Salt and black pepper, to taste
- 4 teaspoons hoisin sauce
- 4 teaspoons rice vinegar
- 4 tablespoons of brown sugar
- 4 cups beef broth

Directions

1. Sterilized the canning jars and prepare the pressure canner according to the manufacturer's instructions.
2. Rub meat with salt and black pepper.
3. Brown the beef pieces in the skillet from each side.
4. Combine the hoisin sauce, rice vinegar, and brown sugar in a bowl; mix it all well.
5. Place the beef pieces in a large bowl or Ziploc bag.
6. Pour the marinade over the meat.
7. Marinate in the refrigerator overnight.
8. Preheat your pressure canner according to the manufacturer's instructions.
9. Remove the beef from the bag and place them in sterilized canning jars, leaving about 1-inch of headspace.
10. Pour the beef broth into each jar, leaving 1-inch of headspace.
11. Remove any air bubbles and clean the jars.
12. Put lids on top and seal the jar.
13. Close the canner lid and bring it to the recommended pressure for your altitude.
14. Process the jars at the specified pressure and time according to recommended guidelines for canning beef.
15. Remove jars, let them get cool completely, check the seal, and let it get cool.
16. Store it in a cool, dark place.

Nutrition Facts: Calories: 456 | Total Fat: 14.8g | Saturated Fat: 5.5g | Sodium: 490mg

Carbohydrate: 4.8g | Sugars: 4.4g | Protein: 70.8g

Stews, Soups, Casseroles, and Broth Recipes

Guide Table For Soups

Table 1. Recommended process time for **Soups** in a dial-gauge pressure canner.						
			Canner Pressure (PSI) at Altitudes			
Style of Pack	**Jar Size**	**Process Time**	**0 - 2,000 ft**	**2,001 - 4,000 ft**	**4,001 - 6,000 ft**	**6,001 - 8,000 ft**
Hot	Pints	60* min	**11 lb**	12 lb	13 lb	14 lb
	Quarts	75*	**11**	12	13	14
* Caution: Process for 100 minutes if soup contains seafood.						

Table 2. Recommended process time for **Soups** in a weighted-gauge pressure canner				
			Canner Pressure (PSI) at Altitudes of	
Style of Pack	**Jar Size**	**Process Time**	**0 - 1,000 ft**	**Above 1,000 ft**
Hot	Pints	60* min	**10 lb**	15 lb
	Quarts	75*	**10**	15
* Caution: Process for 100 minutes if soup contains seafood.				

Guide Table For Meat Stock/Broth

Table 1. Recommended process time for **Meat Stock** in a dial-gauge pressure canner.						
			Canner Pressure (PSI) at Altitudes of			
Style of Pack	**Jar Size**	**Process Time**	**0 - 2,000 ft**	**2,001 - 4,000 ft**	**4,001 - 6,000 ft**	**6,001 - 8,000 ft**
Hot	Pints	20 min	**11 lb**	12 lb	13 lb	14 lb
	Quarts	25	**11**	12	13	14

Table 2. Recommended process time for **Meat Stock** in a weighted-gauge pressure canner.				
			Canner Pressure (PSI) at Altitudes of	
Style of Pack	**Jar Size**	**Process Time**	**0 - 1,000 ft**	**Above 1,000 ft**
Hot	Pints	20 min	**10 lb**	15 lb
	Quarts	25	**10**	15

Lamb Stew With Potatoes

Yield: 4 Servings

Preparation Time: 35-45 Minutes (Excluding Canning Time)

Ingredients

- 2 pounds lamb, cut into pieces about 1-inch
- 1 onion, chopped
- 2 cloves of garlic, minced
- 2 carrots, sliced
- 2 potatoes, diced
- 4 cups beef or vegetable broth
- 1 teaspoon dried thyme
- Salt and pepper to taste

Directions

1. Sterilized the canning jars and prepare the pressure canner according to the manufacturer's instructions.
2. Take a Dutch oven, add meat, and brown over medium heat.
3. Next, combine the onion and garlic in the pot and cook until the aroma comes.
4. Next, add the carrots, diced potatoes, beef, broth, thyme, salt, and pepper.
5. Let it boil and simmer for 15 minutes.
6. Ladle the stew into sterilized jars, leaving about 1-inch of headspace.
7. Take a plastic spatula and gently insert it into the jar along the inside edge.
8. Run it up and down between the food and the jar to release any air bubbles.
9. Close the jars with sterilized lids and process them in a pressure canner according to the manufacturer's instructions for lamb stew.
10. After canning, let the jars cool and check the seals.
11. Store it in a cool, dark place.

Nutrition Facts

Calories: 560 | Total Fat: 18.2g | Saturated Fat: 6.4g | Sodium: 964mg

Carbohydrate: 23.9g | Sugars: 4.6g | Protein: 71g

Lamb Stew With Carrots

Yield: 4 Servings

Preparation Time: 35-45 Minutes (Excluding Canning Time)

Ingredients

- 2 teaspoons of vegetable oil
- 2 pounds lamb cut into 1-inch cubes
- 1 onion, chopped
- 2 celery stalks, chopped
- 2 carrots, sliced
- 2 cloves of garlic, minced
- 1 cup diced tomatoes
- 4 cups beef or vegetable broth
- 1 teaspoon dried rosemary
- Salt and pepper to taste

Directions

1. Sterilized the canning jars and prepare the pressure canner according to the manufacturer's instructions.
2. Heat the oil and brown meat over medium heat in a cooking pot.
3. Add onion, celery, carrots, and minced garlic; cook until softened.
4. Stir in diced tomatoes, broth, rosemary, salt, and pepper.
5. Let it boil and then simmer for 20 minutes.
6. Transfer stew to sterilized jars, leaving 1-inch of headspace.
7. Remove air bubbles using a plastic spatula and gently insert it into the jar along the inside edge.
8. Run it up and down between the food and the jar to release any air bubbles.
9. Seal jars with sterilized lids and process in a pressure canner per instructions for lamb stew.
10. Allow jars to cool, check seals, and store in a cool, dark place.

Nutrition Facts

Calories: 517 | Total Fat: 20.5g | Saturated Fat: 6.8g | Sodium: 967mg

Carbohydrate: 9.2g | Sugars: 4.7g | Protein: 69.7g

Classic Veal Stew

Yield: 4 Servings

Preparation Time: 35 Minutes (Excluding Canning Time)

Ingredients

- 2 pounds of veal meat, cut into cubes
- 2 cloves of garlic, minced
- 1 onion, chopped
- 1 cup frozen peas
- 2 potatoes, diced
- 2 celery stalks, chopped
- 2 carrots, sliced
- 4 cups beef broth
- 1 teaspoon dried thyme
- Salt and pepper to taste

Directions

1. Sterilized the canning jars and prepare the pressure canner according to the manufacturer's instructions.
2. Brown the veal meat cubes in olive oil over low heat in a large pot.
3. Add minced garlic and onion and let it sauté until aroma comes.
4. Add frozen peas, diced potatoes, chopped celery, sliced carrots, beef or vegetable broth, dried thyme, salt, and pepper. Sit well.
5. Let stew boil and then simmer for 20 minutes.
6. Transfer the stew to sterilized jars, leaving 1-inch headspace.
7. Take a plastic spatula and gently insert it into the jar along the inside edge.
8. Run it up and down between the food and the jar to release any air bubbles.
9. Seal the jars with sanitized lids and process them in a pressure canner according to the manufacturer's instructions.
10. Once canned, allow the jars to cool, check the seals, and store them in a cool, dark place.

Nutrition Facts

Calories: 609 | Total Fat: 18.9g | Saturated Fat: 8.2g | Sodium: 1020mg

Carbohydrate: 29.8g | Sugars: 6.6g | Protein: 75.6g

Meat with Beets

Yield: 4 Servings

Preparation Time: 35 -45 Minutes (Excluding Canning Time)

Ingredients

- 2 pounds of meat (such as beef or venison), cut into 1-inch pieces
- 1 onion, chopped
- 2 cloves of garlic, minced
- 2 pounds of beets, peeled and cut into desired sizes (slices or cubes)
- 4 cups beef or vegetable broth
- Salt and pepper to taste

Directions

1. Sterilized the canning jars and prepare the pressure canner according to the manufacturer's instructions.
2. In a large pot, brown the meat pieces over medium heat.
3. Add the onion and garlic.
4. Cook until the aroma comes and the onions are soft.
5. Add the chopped beets and beef or vegetable broth to the pot.
6. Add salt and pepper to taste, and bring the mixture to a boil.
7. Next, lower the heat and simmer it for about 20 minutes.
8. Ladle the meat and beet mixture into sterilized jars, leaving about 1-inch of headspace.
9. Remove air bubbles using a plastic spatula and gently insert it into the jar along the inside edge.
10. Run it up and down between the food and the jar to release any air bubbles.
11. Close the jars with sterilized lids and process them in a pressure canner according to the manufacturer's instructions.
12. The processing time will depend on the type of meat used, so consult the guidelines specific to your meat choice.
13. After canning, let the jars cool and check the seals.
14. Store it in a cool, dark place.

Nutrition Facts

Calories: 551 | Total Fat: 15.1g | Saturated Fat: 5.7g | Sodium: 1108mg

Carbohydrate: 25.8g | Sugars: 19.2g | Protein: 75.8g

Meat and Celery Stew

Yield: 4 Servings

Preparation Time: 35 Minutes (Excluding Canning Time)

Ingredients

- 2 pounds of beef meat, cut into pieces
- 1 onion, chopped
- 1 cup celery, diced
- 2-4 Garlic cloves, minced
- 4 cups vegetable broth
- Salt and pepper to taste

Directions

1. Sterilized the canning jars and prepare the pressure canner according to the manufacturer's instructions.
2. In a Dutch oven, brown the meat pieces over medium heat.
3. Then add the chopped vegetables and minced garlic.
4. Cook until slightly softened.
5. Add vegetable broth to cover the meat and vegetables.
6. Season if liked with salt and pepper.
7. Bring the stew to a boil, and simmer for about 10 minutes, covered.
8. Ladle the meat stew into sterilized jars, ensuring 1-inch of headspace.
9. Remove air bubbles using a plastic spatula and gently insert it into the jar along the inside edge.
10. Run it up and down between the food and the jar to release any air bubbles.
11. Close the jars with sterilized lids and process them in a pressure canner according to the manufacturer's instructions.
12. Typically, meat stews are processed at 10-11 pounds of pressure for 75 minutes (pints) or 90 minutes (quarts).
13. After canning, let the jars cool and check the seals.
14. Store in a cool, dark place.

Nutrition Facts

Calories: 477 | Total Fat: 15.6g | Saturated Fat: 5.7g | Sodium: 934mg

Carbohydrate: 4.8g | Sugars: 2.2g | Protein: 74.2g

Vegetable Soup

Yield: 10 Servings

Preparation Time: 30-40 Minutes (Excluding Canning Time)

Ingredients

- 8 cups peeled tomatoes, chopped cored
- 6 cups potatoes, cubed and peeled
- 6 cups thickly sliced carrots
- 4 cups lima beans, cooked
- 4 cups fresh corn kernels
- 2 cups celery, sliced
- 2 cups onions, chopped
- 6 cups water
- Salt and ground black pepper

Directions

1. First, sterilize the jars.
2. Now cook the vegetables.
3. Combine tomatoes, potatoes, carrots, beans, corn, celery, onions, and water in a large pot or a saucepan.
4. Let it boil over medium heat, then reduce the heat.
5. Simmer it for 15 minutes.
6. Season it with salt and pepper.
7. Fill each jar with soup using a funnel, leaving 1-1/2 inches of headspace.
8. Remove air bubbles from the jars and maintain 1-inch headspace.
9. Dampen a clean paper towel with vinegar and wipe the rims of the jars.
10. Extract the lids from hot water and place them on the cleaned rims using a jar lifter. Add rings to the tops of each jar and turn them to seal "finger tight."
11. Add jars to the pressure canner.
12. Adjust pressure and time for altitude if necessary.
13. Once the processing time is complete, turn off the flame.
14. Remove the canner lid after 10 minutes, then carefully lift out the jars and place them on a dishtowel where they are undisturbed overnight to cool.
15. Store it in a cool, dark place.

Nutrition Facts: Calories: 219 | Total Fat: 1.4g | Saturated Fat: 0.3g | Sodium: 195mg

Carbohydrate: 45.4g | Sugars: 7.8g | Protein: 9g

Canning Split Pea Soup

Yield: 2 Servings

Preparation Time: 30 Minutes (Excluding Canning Time)

Ingredients

- 1 pound of split peas, dry and packed
- 2 cups vegetable broth
- 3 medium carrots, sliced
- 1 cup onion, chopped
- ½ tablespoon allspice
- 1 cup cooked ham, diced
- 1 bay leaf
- Salt and pepper to taste

Directions

1. First, sterilize the jars.
2. Add split peas and two quarts of water or broth in a Dutch oven.
3. Let it boil, and then lower the heat.
4. Simmer it for 1 hour.
5. Add carrots and onions to the Dutch oven.
6. Add all the spices and bay leaves listed in the recipe.
7. Preheat your pressure canner for hot pack canning, following the manufacturer's instructions.
8. Simmer the soup for 30 minutes until the vegetables are fully cooked. Remove the bay leaf if used.
9. Fill the canning jars with ham.
10. Ladle the split pea soup into prepared canning jars, leaving 1-inch of headspace.
11. Remove air bubbles.
12. Seal the jars with two-part canning lids, tightening them to finger tight.
13. Load the canning jars into the canner and close the lid.
14. Process the jars in a canner, and adjust accordingly to your altitude.
15. Once the processing time is complete, turn off the heat.
16. Allow the canner to cool down.
17. After cooling, remove the jars from the canner and check the seals.
18. Store it in a cool, dark place.

Nutrition Facts: Calories: 986 | Total Fat: 10g | Saturated Fat: 2.8g | Sodium: 1744mg
Carbohydrate: 155.9g | Sugars: 25.8g | Protein: 73.2g

Mushroom Soup Base

Yield: 6 Servings

Preparation Time: 30-40Minutes (Excluding Canning Time)

Ingredients

- 8 cups of minced onions (about 2 1/4 pounds)
- 6 cloves of garlic, minced
- 2 pounds of mushrooms, thinly sliced
- 1 cup of dry white wine
- 8 cups beef broth
- 2 tablespoons of non-iodized salt
- 1 teaspoon of ground black pepper
- 1 tablespoon of dried thyme

Directions

1. Sterilize the canning jars.
2. Heat the canner on low heat to preheat it.
3. Melt the butter and sauté the onions and garlic in a Dutch oven for about 15 minutes.
4. Add the mushrooms and continue sautéing for 10 minutes.
5. Stir in the wine, broth, salt, black pepper, and thyme.
6. Bring the mixture to a boil for five minutes.
7. Remove the Dutch oven from heat and ladle the soup into hot jars.
8. Start with the solids, then distribute the liquid evenly among the jars, leaving 1-inch of headspace.
9. Remove air bubbles, and adjust the headspace by 1-inch.
10. Wipe the rims of the canning jars and tighten the bands until they are fingertip tight.
11. Put the jars into the pressure canner.
12. Adjust the processing time and pressure for altitude.
13. Allow the canner to depressurize naturally after the designated processing time.
14. Take out the jars and let them cool.
15. Check the seals.
16. Store the jars for up to 12 months in a cool, dark place.

Nutrition Facts: Calories: 269 | Total Fat: 12.1g | Saturated Fat: 6.6g | Sodium: 1103mg Carbohydrate: 23.1g | Sugars: 10.4g | Protein: 13.3g

Chicken Tortilla Soup

Yield: 6 Servings

Preparation Time: 30-40 Minutes (Excluding Canning Time)

Ingredients

- 4 large chicken breasts
- 1 cup of carrots, sliced in half-moon shaped
- 1 large onion, diced
- 16 Roma tomatoes, diced
- 2 cups dried black beans
- 1 cup mild green chilies, chopped f
- 2 cups of water
- 6 cups chicken stock
- 4 cups corn kernels, fresh cut or frozen and thawed
- 2 teaspoons ground cumin
- 2 teaspoons sea salt
- 2 teaspoons ground chili powder
- ½ tablespoon paprika
- 1/2 tablespoon oregano
- 2-4 dried cayenne peppers
- 8 garlic cloves, minced
- 4 teaspoons of Canning Gel

Directions

1. Sterilize the canning jars.
2. Take a medium or small stainless steel stockpot, add chicken, cover the chicken breasts with 2 inches of water, and boil for 15 minutes.
3. Use canning tongs to remove the chicken and transfer it to a clean cutting board to let it get cool. Discard the water.
4. Cut the chicken into bite-sized pieces once cool.
5. If using dried black beans, ensure they are properly cleaned and rinsed, pre-boil them separately in a saucepan for 15 minutes, drain, rinse, and then add them to the soup.
6. In a pot or Dutch oven, mix all the ingredients and boil over medium-high heat.
7. Boil for 4 minutes, and then add the cooked chicken.
8. Bring it back to a boil and continue boiling gently for 5 minutes.
9. Remove from heat.
10. Use a slotted spoon to remove dried cayenne peppers from the soup and discard them.
11. Use a slotted spoon and funnel to fill the sterilized hot jars over half full with the soup contents, ensuring 1-inch head space.

12. Remove any air bubbles.

13. Use a cloth or kitchen towel dipped in vinegar to wipe the jar rims and screw bands. Place a sterilized lid and ring on top of each jar and hand tighten.

14. Process the jars in a pressure canner.

15. Make sure to adjust the pressure according to your area.

16. Take out the jars, and let them cool.

17. Check the seal.

18. Store it in a cool, dark place.

Nutrition Facts

Calories: 602 | Total Fat: 11.1g | Saturated Fat: 2.7g | Sodium: 1529mg

Carbohydrate: 81.9g | Sugars: 18.6g | Protein: 50.2g

Mexican Soup

Yield: 6 Servings

Preparation Time: 30 Minutes (Excluding Canning Time)

Ingredients

- 3 boneless chicken breasts, cooked and shredded
- 1 ½cups carrots, diced
- 2 cups celery, diced
- 1 large onion, chopped
- 29 ounces Rotel Tomatoes
- 30 ounces of cans of kidney beans, rinsed and drained
- 4 cups diced tomatoes, fresh
- 6 cups water
- 6 cups chicken broth
- 3 cups corn, fresh
- 1 teaspoon ground cumin
- 1 tablespoon canning salt
- 4 garlic cloves (minced)
- 3 chicken bouillon cubes

Directions

1. Sterilize the canning jars
2. Add a generous amount of water to a Dutch oven and add chicken for boiling.
3. Once the chicken has cooled down, shred it. Set it aside.
4. Combine all the ingredients except the shredded chicken in a large pot.
5. Let it boil, cover it, and simmer for 2-3 minutes.
6. Add the chicken and lightly boil for 5 minutes.
7. Pour the hot soup into jars, leaving 1-inch headspace.
8. Remove the air bubbles from the jars and wipe the rims with a wet cloth.
9. Tightly seal the jars and put the jars into the pressure canner.
10. Process quart-sized jars at 11 pounds of pressure for 90 minutes or pint-sized jars for 75 minutes (adjust the processing time and pressure if you are at a higher altitude).
11. Take out the jars from the pressure canner and let them cool for 12 -24 hours.
12. Check the seal; the lids should not flex up and down when pressing from the center.
13. Store it in a cool, dark place.

Nutrition Facts: Calories: 893 | Total Fat: 9.8g | Saturated Fat: 2.4g | Sodium: 2218mg

Carbohydrate: 133.7g | Sugars: 12.2g | Protein: 70.9g

Chicken Soup

Yield: 16 Servings

Preparation Time: 30-35 Minutes (Excluding Canning Time)

Ingredients

- 16 cups chicken stock
- 3 pounds of cooked and diced chicken
- 3 stalks of celery, chopped (
- 3 carrots, sliced
- 1 onion, chopped
- 3 chicken bouillon cubes, optional
- Salt and pepper to taste

Directions

1. Sterilize the canning jars.
2. Next, prepare a pressure canner according to the manufacturer's instructions.
3. Take a Dutch oven and combine all the ingredients in it, and bring them to a boil.
4. Let them simmer for 10 minutes.
5. Using a slotted spoon, distribute the solids evenly among jars.
6. Add broth, leaving 1-inch of headspace.
7. Secure the jars with canning lids, remove any bubbles, and process them in a pressure canner, adjusting according to altitude.
8. Once the canning time is complete, allow the canner to cool.
9. Remove jars.
10. Check the seals and store them.

Nutrition Facts

Calories: 139 | Total Fat: 8.1g | Saturated Fat: 2.4g | Sodium: 946mg

Carbohydrate: 2.8g | Sugars: 1.7g | Protein: 15.2g

Canning Lentil Soup

Yield: 10 Servings

Preparation Time: 60-75 Minutes (Excluding Canning Time)

Ingredients

- 4 cups dried lentils
- 8 cups water
- 2 tablespoons olive oil
- 1 large onion, chopped
- 4 cloves garlic, minced
- 2 carrots, diced
- 2 celery stalks, diced
- 1 can diced tomatoes (14 ounces)
- 1 teaspoon ground cumin
- 1 teaspoon ground coriander
- 1 teaspoon paprika
- 1 bay leaf
- Salt and pepper to taste
- Lemon juice (optional for flavor)

Directions

1. Sterilize the canning jars.
2. Next, prepare a pressure canner according to the manufacturer's instructions.
3. Rinse the lentils thoroughly and remove all the debris.
4. Add them to a large pot and cover with water. Bring water to a boil and cook lentils for about 10 minutes.
5. Then drain and set the lentils aside.
6. Pour the olive oil into a large pot and sauté chopped onion, minced garlic, and sauté until aroma comes over medium flame.
7. Add the carrots and celery, and cook for 5 minutes, stirring occasionally.
8. Put the cooked lentils into the pot and tomatoes. Mix it well.
9. Add the ground cumin, coriander, paprika, bay leaf, salt, and pepper. Mix again.
10. Pour in the water, ensuring that the lentils are fully covered.
11. Bring this to a simmering boil, lower the heat, and cook for 50 minutes, covered.
12. Pour soup into each jar, filling it up to 3/4 inch from the top.
13. Wet a paper towel and use it to wipe the rim of each jar.
14. Close the jars.
15. Carefully put the jars into your pressure canner.
16. Refer to the instructions provided with your canner and follow them accordingly.

17. Once the pressure reaches zero, remove the jars from the canner.

18. Let the canning jars get cool at room temperature.

19. Check the seals.

20. Store jars in a cool, dry place.

Nutrition Facts

Calories: 323 | Total Fat: 3.9g | Saturated Fat: 0.5g | Sodium: 26mg

Carbohydrate: 52.3g | Sugars: 4.8g | Protein: 20.9g

Asparagus Soup

Yield: 10 Servings

Preparation Time: 60-75 Minutes (Excluding Canning Time)

Ingredients

- 2 small sweet onions, diced
- 3-5 celery stalks, diced
- 8-10 garlic cloves, minced
- 2 teaspoons dried tarragon leaves
- 1 tablespoon sea salt (optional)
- ½ teaspoon black pepper
- 3-4 pounds asparagus spears, cut into 1-inch pieces
- 15 cups chicken or vegetable broth
- 2 red tomatoes, diced

Directions

1. Sterilize the canning jars.
2. Next, prepare a pressure canner according to the manufacturer's instructions.
3. In a Dutch oven, melt the butter and sauté the onions, celery, garlic, tarragon, salt, and pepper.
4. Cook on a medium flame for about 8 to 10 minutes.
5. Put in the asparagus and mix well.
6. Cook for 10 minutes, stirring frequently.
7. Pour in the broth and tomatoes.
8. Let the boil come, then reduce the heat and cook for 1 hour.
9. Let the soup cool and process it in batches using a food processor.
10. Ladle the hot soup into jars, leaving a one-inch headspace.
11. Remove air bubbles.
12. Use a wet kitchen cloth to wipe the jar rims. Add lids and rings, and hand tightens them.
13. Process the jars in your pressure canner according to altitude.
14. Allow the jars to cool.
15. Remove the jars, check the seal, then store them in a cool, dark place.

Nutrition Facts

Calories: 437 | Total Fat: 11.8g | Saturated Fat: 4.9g | Sodium: 561mg

Carbohydrate: 11.9g | Sugars: 5.4g | Protein: 69.8g

Tomato Soup Concentrate

Yield: 30 Servings

Preparation Time: 2-3 Hours (Excluding Canning Time)

Ingredients

- 15 pounds of tomatoes
- 2 cups diced onion
- 2 tablespoons granulated garlic
- 1 tablespoon dried Italian seasoning
- 1 tablespoon salt plus more to taste
- 2 1/2 teaspoons citric acid

Directions

1. Sterilize the canning jars.
2. Next, prepare a pressure canner according to the manufacturer's instructions.
3. In a Dutch oven or pot, combine the tomatoes and diced onions.
4. Add approximately a cup of water to the pot and let it boil.
5. Cook the mixture for about an hour, stirring occasionally.
6. Remove the pot from the stove. Place a food mill with its finest screen over a heatproof bowl.
7. In batches, pass the cooked tomatoes and onions through the food mill.
8. Once all the tomatoes are milled, add the garlic and Italian seasoning to the pot.
9. Put the pot back on the flame and let it boil.
10. Cook for 1-3 hours until the soup concentrate has reduced by one-third.
11. Season it with salt to taste.
12. Divide the citric acid evenly among canning jars.
13. Pour the finished soup concentrate into the jars using a funnel, leaving a half-inch headspace.
14. Wipe the rims of the jars.
15. Close the jars, and process them in your pressure canner.
16. Adjust the processing time and pressure based on altitude.
17. Once done, remove the jars,
18. Let the jars get cool, and check the seal.
19. Store it in a cool, dark place.

Nutrition Facts: Calories: 47 | Total Fat: 0.6g | Saturated Fat: 0.1g | Sodium: 12mg

Carbohydrate: 10g | Sugars: 6.5g | Protein: 2.2g

Chilli Tomato Vegetable Soup

Yield: 16 Servings

Preparation Time: 30 Minutes (Excluding Canning Time)

Ingredients

- 24 small plum tomatoes, chopped
- 2 cups tomatillos, chopped
- 1 cup onion, chopped
- 1 cup carrots peeled, sliced
- 1 cup red pepper, chopped
- 1 cup green bell pepper, chopped and seeded
- 2 ounces hot pepper seeded and chopped
- 6 cups whole kernel corn, uncooked
- 2 tablespoon chili powder
- 2 teaspoons cayenne pepper
- 1 teaspoon ground black pepper
- 1 teaspoon salt
- 1 tablespoon hot sauce
- 5 cups tomato juice
- 2 cups water

Directions

1. Sterilize the canning jars.
2. Next, prepare a pressure canner according to the manufacturer's instructions.
3. Take a large pot and add chop tomatoes.
4. Husk, the tomatillos, wash them well, and then chop.
5. Then add it to the pot.
6. Add onion, carrots, and all the peppers to the pot.
7. Next, add corn and all remaining ingredients to the pot.
8. Bring to a boil, then lower heat to a simmer for 15 minutes.
9. Fill each jar halfway with solids, and then top up with liquid.
10. Leave 1-inch headspace.
11. Remove any air bubbles from the jar.
12. Wipe the rims of the jars and close them tightly.
13. Process the jars in your pressure canner according to altitude.
14. Once the processing is complete, carefully remove the jars from the canner. Allow the jars to cool naturally.

15. Check the seals of the jars to ensure they are properly sealed. If any jars do not seal correctly, refrigerate them for immediate use.
16. Store the sealed and properly cooled jars in a suitable location for long-term storage.

Nutrition Facts

Calories: 108 | Total Fat: 1.5g | Saturated Fat: 0.2g | Sodium: 413mg

Carbohydrate: 23.6g | Sugars: 10.5g | Protein: 4.6g

Chicken Soup with Celery

Yield: 8 Servings

Preparation Time: 2 Hours (Excluding Canning Time)

Ingredients

- 4 pounds of chicken, cut into pieces
- 16 cups water
- 2.4 stalks celery
- 2 white onions, quartered
- 2 teaspoons salt
- 1 tablespoon peppercorns
- 2 bay leaves

Directions

1. Sterilize the canning jars.
2. Add the canning jars to simmering water to heat them until ready; avoid boiling them.
3. In a large Dutch oven, combine chicken and water and bring it to a boil.
4. Put the remaining ingredients in the Dutch oven and bring it back to a boil.
5. Reduce the heat and simmer for about 2 hours.
6. Turn off the flame and skim off any accumulated foam on the surface.
7. Ladle the hot chicken soup into hot jars, leaving 1-inch headspace.
8. Remove air bubbles and Wipe the rim clean.
9. Place the hot lids in the center of each jar and apply the bands, adjusting them until they are fingertip tight.
10. Add the filled jars to the pressure canner.
11. Adjust the processing time and pressure based on your altitude and follows your pressure canner's instructions.
12. Allow the jars to cool in the canner for 10 minutes, and then carefully remove them.
13. Once cooled, check the lids for a proper seal after 24 hours.
14. The lid should be properly sealed.
15. Store it in a cool, dark place.

Nutrition Facts: Calories: 356 | Total Fat: 6.9g | Saturated Fat: 1.9g | Sodium: 744mg

Carbohydrate: 3.2g | Sugars: 1.3g | Protein: 66.2g

Beef Broth

Yield: 10 Servings

Preparation Time: 5 Hours (Excluding Canning Time)

Ingredients

- 5 pounds of beef stock bones
- 6 whole onions, quartered, skins included
- 6 carrots, roughly chopped
- 4 celery ribs, roughly chopped
- 1 head of garlic cut in half
- Water; cover the ingredients by about 2 inches
- 3 bay leaves
- 1 teaspoon dried thyme
- 3 sprigs of fresh rosemary
- 1 teaspoon of dried parsley
- 1 teaspoon of black pepper

Directions

1. Preheat your oven to 400 degrees F.
2. Add the beef bones to a large roasting pan.
3. Roast them for 45 minutes, turning them once halfway through.
4. Remove the roasting pan from the oven.
5. Transfer the bones to a large stockpot.
6. Pour 1 cup of water into the roasting pan to deglaze it, scrap any brown bits from the bottom, and add this liquid to the stockpot.
7. Add the vegetables and aromatics to the stockpot.
8. Cover the ingredients with water, ensuring it is about 2 inches above the contents.
9. Let it boil, and then reduce the heat to a simmer.
10. Allow it to simmer from 4 to 24 hours.
11. Once the broth is done cooking, place a colander lined with folded cheesecloth over another large stockpot.
12. Carefully scoop the contents of the beef broth stockpot into the colander, allowing the liquid to strain into the other stockpot.
13. Remove air bubbles.
14. Prepare a dial-gauge or weighted-gauge pressure canner, along with jars and lids.
15. Keep the jars warm in the prepared pressure canner while bringing the finished broth to a boil.

16. Carefully spoon the hot broth into each jar using a canning funnel, leaving 1-inch headspace.

17. Apply the lids and rings, and clean the jars with a damp cloth before placing them back in the canner.

18. Adjust processing time based on your altitude.

19. Once the processing time is complete, allow the canner to depressurize naturally.

20. Using a jar lifter, carefully transfer the hot jars to a clean surface, leaving 1-inch of space between each jar.

21. Let the jars cool to room temperature over the next 12 to 24 hours, and check the seal on each lid.

22. Store in a cool, dry place.

Nutrition Facts

Calories: 538 | Total Fat: 36.2g | Saturated Fat: 14.1g | Sodium: 146mg

Carbohydrate: 3.8g | Sugars: 1.8g | Protein: 46.5g

Pork Broth

Yield: 12 Servings

Preparation Time: 6-7 Hours (Excluding Canning Time)

Ingredients

- 6 pounds of pork bones (neck bones, ribs, or any other bones suitable for broth)
- 1 large onion, quartered
- 2 carrots, roughly chopped
- 2 celery stalks, roughly chopped
- 4 garlic cloves smashed
- 2 bay leaves
- 1 tablespoon black peppercorns
- Water

Directions

1. Combine the pork bones, onion, carrots, celery, garlic, bay leaves, and black peppercorns in a large stockpot.
2. Add water to cover all the ingredients and let it boil.
3. Allow it to simmer for about 4 to 6 hours.
4. After simmering, remove the stockpot from the heat and let it cool slightly.
5. Prepare a large bowl or pot with a colander lined with cheesecloth.
6. Carefully pour the broth through the colander, straining out the solids and leaving only the liquid.
7. Discard the bones and vegetables.
8. Sterilize the canning jars.
9. Place the jars in the canner or a large pot filled with water.
10. Heat them until ready for use, but do not bring them to a boil.
11. Heat the strained pork broth in a separate pot until it boils gently.
12. Carefully spoon the hot broth into each jar using a canning funnel, leaving 1-inch headspace.
13. Clean the jar rims with a damp cloth.
14. Add the lids on the jars and screw on the rings.
15. Put the canning jars in the prepared pressure canner, following the manufacturer's instructions.

16. Adjust the processing time and pressure based on your altitude.

17. Once the processing time is complete, carefully remove the jars from the canner.

18. Let the jars cool completely for 24 hours.

19. Check the seals and store them in a cool, dark place.

Nutrition Facts

Calories: 843 | Total Fat: 52.2g | Saturated Fat: 18.1g | Sodium: 261mg

Carbohydrate: 0g | Sugars: 0g | Protein: 92.3g

Lamb Bone Broth

Yield: 10 Servings

Preparation Time: 6-7 Hours (Excluding Canning Time)

Ingredients

- 5-6 pounds of lamb bones (such as neck bones or shanks)
- Water

Directions

1. Place the lamb bones in a large stockpot.
2. Pour water to cover the bones.
3. Let it boil, and then reduce the heat to a simmer.
4. Allow the lamb bones to simmer for about 4 to 6 hours.
5. After simmering, remove the stockpot from the heat and let it cool slightly.
6. Set up a pot with a colander lined with cheesecloth.
7. Carefully pour the broth through the colander, removing bone fragments or impurities and leaving only the liquid.
8. Sterilize the canning jars.
9. Heat the strained lamb broth in a separate pot until it boils gently.
10. Carefully spoon the hot broth into each sterilized jar using a canning funnel, leaving 1-inch headspace.
11. Clean the jar rims with a damp cloth.
12. Add the lids to the jars and screw tightly.
13. Place the filled jars in the pressure canner, following the manufacturer's instructions for water levels and processing times.
14. Adjust the processing time and pressure based on your altitude.
15. Once the processing time is complete.
16. Remove the jars from the canner, and let them cool.
17. Check the seal of the jars and store them in a cool and dark place.

Nutrition Facts: Calories: 422 | Total Fat: 16.6g | Saturated Fat: 5.9g | Sodium: 172mg
Carbohydrate: 0g | Sugars: 0g | Protein: 63.7g

Beef Bone Broth

Yield: 12 Servings

Preparation Time: 8-12 Hours (Excluding Canning Time)

Ingredients

- 5-6 pounds of beef bones (such as marrow bones or knuckle bones)
- Water

Directions

1. Preheat your oven to 40-450 degrees F.
2. Add the beef bones to a roasting pan and roast in the oven for 55 minutes, flipping halfway.
3. Transfer the bones to a large stockpot once cooked.
4. Deglaze the bottom of the roasting pan by adding 1 cup of water and scraping up any browned bits. Pour the liquid and browned bits into the stockpot with the bones.
5. Add enough water to the stockpot to cover the bones, but do not exceed the maximum fill line of your pressure canner.
6. Bring the mixture to a boil.
7. Reduce the heat and simmer.
8. Allow the beef bones to simmer for about 8 to 12 hours.
9. This long simmering time helps extract the flavors and nutrients from the bones.
10. After simmering, remove the stockpot from the heat and let it cool slightly.
11. Set up a large bowl with a colander lined with cheesecloth.
12. Carefully pour the broth through the colander, removing bone fragments or impurities and leaving only the liquid.
13. Prepare a dial-gauge or weighted-gauge pressure canner according to the manufacturer's instructions.
14. Sterilize the canning jars.
15. Place the jars in the canner or a large pot filled with water. Heat them until ready for use, but do not bring them to a boil.
16. Heat the strained beef bone broth in a separate pot until it boils gently.
17. Carefully spoon the hot broth into each jar using a canning funnel, leaving 1-inch headspace.
18. Wipe the canning jar rims with a damp cloth.

19. Top the lids on the jars and screw the lid tightly.

20. Place the filled jars in the pressure canner, following the manufacturer's instructions for water levels and processing times.

21. Adjust the processing time and pressure based on your altitude.

22. Once the processing time is complete,

23. Remove the jars from the canner.

24. Place them on a heat-resistant surface.

25. Let the jars cool completely.

26. Check the seal.

27. Store them in a cool, dark place.

Nutrition Facts

Calories: 509 | Total Fat: 20.5g | Saturated Fat: 7.4g | Sodium: 155mg

Carbohydrate: 18.1g | Sugars: 3.2g | Protein: 59.9g

Moroccan Lamb Soup

Yield: 4 Servings

Preparation Time: 20-40 Minutes (Excluding Canning Time)

Ingredients

- 1 pound lamb, diced
- 1 onion, chopped
- 2 cloves garlic, minced
- 2 carrots, diced
- 2 potatoes, diced
- 1 can chickpeas, drained
- 1 can diced tomatoes
- 4 cups lamb or vegetable broth
- 1 teaspoon cumin
- 1 teaspoon paprika
- 1/2 teaspoon cinnamon
- Salt and pepper to taste

Directions

1. In a Dutch oven, brown the lamb pieces over medium to low flame.
2. Put the onions and garlic, and cook until aroma comes.
3. Add carrots, potatoes, chickpeas, diced tomatoes, lamb broth, cumin, paprika, cinnamon, salt, and pepper.
4. Ladle the soup into a sterilized canning jar, ensuring 1-inch headspace.
5. Place the jars into the canner.
6. The process is at the recommended pressure and time according to altitude.
7. Allow the canner to cool naturally, and then remove the jars.
8. Store the jar after checking the seal in a cool, dark place.

Nutrition Facts

Calories: 808 | Total Fat: 24.2g | Saturated Fat: 6.6g | Sodium: 848mg

Carbohydrate: 66.9g | Sugars: 12.1g | Protein: 79.1g

Lamb and Vegetable Soup

Yield: 6 Servings

Preparation Time: 20-40 Minutes (Excluding Canning Time)

Ingredients

- 2 pounds lamb leg, diced
- 1 onion, chopped
- 2 cloves garlic, minced
- 2 potatoes, diced
- 2 carrots, diced
- 2 zucchinis, diced
- 1 can diced tomatoes
- 4 cups lamb or vegetable broth
- 1 teaspoon dried oregano
- 1 teaspoon dried thyme
- 1 bay leaf
- Salt and pepper to taste

Directions

1. In a stock pot, brown the lamb cubes over medium heat.
2. Put the onion and garlic, and sauté until translucent.
3. Add the potatoes, carrots, zucchini, diced tomatoes, lamb broth, oregano, thyme, bay leaf, salt, and pepper.
4. Once the soup is done, spoon it into sterilized canning jars, ensuring 1-inch head space.
5. Process in canner by making altitude adjustments accordingly.
6. Allow the canner to cool naturally, and then remove the jars.
7. Store the jar after checking the seal in a cool, dark place.

Nutrition Facts

Calories: 1045 | Total Fat: 36.2g | Saturated Fat: 12.9g | Sodium: 385mg
Carbohydrate: 18.8g | Sugars: 4.5g | Protein: 152.7g

Rustic Lamb Soup

Yield: 4 Servings

Preparation Time: 20-30 Minutes (Excluding Canning Time)

Ingredients

- 2 pounds lamb shoulder, cubed
- 1 onion, chopped
- 3 cloves garlic, minced
- 2 parsnips, peeled and diced
- 2 turnips, peeled and diced
- 2 carrots, diced
- 2 potatoes, diced
- 4 cups lamb or vegetable broth
- 4 cups water
- 1 bay leaf
- 1 teaspoon dried rosemary
- 1 teaspoon dried thyme
- Salt and pepper to taste

Directions

1. In a Dutch oven, brown the lamb cubes over medium heat.
2. Add the onion and garlic, and sauté until fragrant.
3. Add the parsnips, turnips, carrots, potatoes, lamb broth, water, bay leaf, rosemary, thyme, salt, and pepper.
4. Ladle the soup into a sterilized canning jar, ensuring 1-inch headspace.
5. Place the jars into the canner.
6. The process is at the recommended pressure and time according to altitude.
7. Allow the canner to cool naturally, and then remove the jars.
8. Store the jar after checking the seal in a cool, dark place.

Nutrition Facts

Calories: 592 | Total Fat: 17.1g | Saturated Fat: 6g | Sodium: 255mg

Carbohydrate: 39.4g | Sugars: 9.6g | Protein: 67.6g

Lamb and Chickpea Soup

Yield: 4 Servings

Preparation Time: 20-30 Minutes (Excluding Canning Time)

Ingredients

- 2 pounds of lamb stew meat, cubed
- 1 onion, chopped
- 3 cloves garlic, minced
- 2 carrots, diced
- 2 zucchinis, diced
- 1 can chickpeas, drained and rinsed
- 1 can diced tomatoes
- 4 cups lamb or vegetable broth
- 2 teaspoons ground cumin
- 1 teaspoon ground coriander
- 1/2 teaspoon ground cinnamon
- 1/2 teaspoon ground ginger
- Salt and pepper to taste

Directions

1. In a Dutch oven, brown the lamb cubes over medium heat.
2. Dump the onion and garlic, and sauté until fragrant.
3. Add the carrots, zucchini, chickpeas, diced tomatoes, lamb broth, cumin, coriander, cinnamon, ginger, salt, and pepper.
4. Ladle the soup into a sterilized canning jar, ensuring 1-inch headspace.
5. Place the jars into the canner.
6. The process is at the recommended pressure and time according to altitude.
7. Allow the canner to cool naturally, and then remove the jars.
8. Store the jar after checking the seal in a cool, dark place.

Nutrition Facts

Calories: 1690 | Total Fat: 70g | Saturated Fat: 25.3g | Sodium: 557mg

Carbohydrate: 42.5g | Sugars: 11g | Protein: 211.5g

Lamb Soup with Leeks

Yield: 4 Servings

Preparation Time: 20-30 Minutes (Excluding Canning Time)

Ingredients

- 2 pounds of lamb stew meat, cubed
- 2-3 leeks, white and light green parts sliced
- 3 cloves garlic, minced
- 2 large carrots, diced
- 2 stalks of celery, diced
- 1 can diced tomatoes
- 6 cups lamb broth
- 2 cups water
- 1 teaspoon dried thyme
- 1 bay leaf
- Salt and pepper to taste

Directions

1. In a Dutch oven, brown the lamb stew meat over medium flame.
2. Now put the leeks and garlic, and sauté until the aroma comes.
3. Add the carrots, celery, diced tomatoes, lamb broth, water, thyme, bay leaf, salt, and pepper.
4. Let it simmer and let cook for 10 minutes.
5. Remove it from the heat and ladle the soup into sterilized canning jars, leaving 1-inch headspace at the top.
6. Remove any air bubbles with a plastic utensil or bubble remover tool.
7. Wipe the jar rims, and close the jars.
8. Place the jars inside the pressure canner.
9. Secure the lid on the pressure canner and bring it to high pressure according to the manufacturer's instructions.
10. The process at 10 pounds of pressure for 75 minutes for pint jars (adjust for altitude if needed).
11. After processing, turn off the heat and let the pressure canner cool naturally.
12. Once the canner is safe to open, carefully remove the jars using canning jar tongs.
13. Place the jars on a towel-lined surface to cool, and check for proper seals afterward.
14. Store it in a cool, dark place.

Nutrition Facts: Calories: 1181 | Total Fat: 40.7g | Saturated Fat: 15g | Sodium: 469mg Carbohydrate: 11g | Sugars: 3.6g | Protein: 181.1g

Pork Recipes

Guide Table For Pork

Table 1. Recommended process time for **Ground or Chopped Meat** in a dial-gauge pressure canner.						
			Canner Pressure (PSI) at Altitudes of			
Style of Pack	**Jar Size**	**Process Time**	**0 - 2,000 ft**	**2,001 - 4,000 ft**	**4,001 - 6,000 ft**	**6,001 - 8,000 ft**
Hot	Pints	75 min	**11 lb**	12 lb	13 lb	14 lb
	Quarts	90	**11**	12	13	14

Table 2. Recommended process time for **Ground or Chopped Meat** in a weighted-gauge pressure canner.				
			Canner Pressure (PSI) at Altitudes of	
Style of Pack	**Jar Size**	**Process Time**	**0 - 1,000 ft**	**Above 1,000 ft**
Hot	Pints	75 min	**10 lb**	15 lb
	Quarts	90	**10**	15

Table 3. Recommended process time for **Strips, Cubes, or Chunks of Meat** in a dial-gauge pressure canner.

			Canner Pressure (PSI) at Altitudes of			
Style of Pack	Jar Size	Process Time	0 - 2,000 ft	2,001 - 4,000 ft	4,001 - 6,000 ft	6,001 - 8,000 ft
Hot and Raw	Pints	75 min	**11 lb**	12 lb	13 lb	14 lb
	Quarts	90	**11**	12	13	14

Table 4. Recommended process time for **Strips, Cubes, or Chunks of Meat** in a weighted-gauge pressure canner.

			Canner Pressure (PSI) at Altitudes of	
Style of Pack	Jar Size	Process Time	0 - 1,000 ft	Above 1,000 ft
Hot and Raw	Pints	75 min	**10 lb**	15 lb
	Quarts	90	**10**	15

Pressure Canned Pork

Yield: 4 Servings

Preparation Time: 60 Minutes (Excluding Canning Time)

Ingredients

- 2 pounds of pork
- Oil spray for greasing
- Water to fill jars
- Pickling salt (optional)

Directions

1. Sterilize the canning jars.
2. Next, prepare a pressure canner according to the manufacturer's instructions.
3. Remove bones and trim off excess fat and any gristle.
4. Cut meat into pieces about 1-inch.
5. Spray a skillet with cooking spray.
6. In batches, brown meat is in the skillet.
7. Transfer browned meat to a pot to keep it hot.
8. Pack the meat into sterilized jars.
9. Leave 1-inch headspace.
10. [Optional]: add ½ teaspoon of pickling salt to half-liter (1 US pint) jars; 1 teaspoon of pickling salt to 1 liter (1 US quart) jars.
11. Top jars up with a boiling liquid (water), maintaining 1-inch headspace.
12. Remove bubbles and adjust the headspace.
13. Wipe jar rims.
14. Put lids on.
15. Following the manufacturer's instructions, put the canning jars in the prepared pressure canner.
16. Adjust the processing time and pressure based on your altitude.
17. Once the processing time is complete, carefully remove the jars from the canner.
18. Let the jars cool completely for 24 hours.
19. Check the seals and store them in a cool, dark place.

Nutrition Facts: Calories: 326 | Total Fat: 8.1g | Saturated Fat: 2.7g | Sodium: 129mg
Carbohydrate: 0g | Sugars: 0g | Protein: 59.4g

Homemade Canned Pork

Yield: 4 Servings

Preparation Time: 2 -3 Hours (Excluding Canning Time)

Ingredients

- 2 pounds of pork butt, fat trimmed off
- 1/2 teaspoon curing salt
- 1 1/2 teaspoon kosher salt
- 1/2 teaspoon allspice
- 1/2 teaspoon black pepper
- 1 clove garlic, minced
- 3 bay leaves
- 4 tablespoons caramelized onion

Directions

1. Sterilize the canning jars.
2. Next, prepare a pressure canner according to the manufacturer's instructions.
3. Begin by cutting the pork into 1-inch pieces.
4. In a separate bowl, mix the curing salt and kosher salt.
5. Place the pork in a larger bowl and sprinkle it with the kosher salt mixture.
6. Mix the meat well to ensure an even distribution of the seasonings.
7. Cover the bowl and let the pork cure in the refrigerator for 24-48 hours.
8. After the curing time, take the pork out of the fridge and sprinkle it with ground allspice and black pepper.
9. Add the pressed garlic and thoroughly mix everything.
10. Before proceeding, refer to a detailed guide on properly canned meat to ensure safety and proper procedures.
11. Pack the cured and seasoned pork into 16-oz (1 pint) mason jars, making sure not to pack it too tightly. Leave 1/2" headspace at the top of each jar.
12. Add one bay leaf to each jar and top it with one tablespoon of caramelized onion.
13. Remove air bubbles.
14. Wipe the rims of the jars.
15. Place the lids on top of each jar and screw on the bands finger-tight.
16. Prepare a pressure canner and process the jars.
17. Following the manufacturer's instructions, put the canning jars in the prepared pressure canner.
18. Adjust the processing time and pressure based on your altitude.

19. Once the processing time is complete, carefully remove the jars from the canner.

20. Let the jars cool completely for 24 hours.

21. Check the seals and store them in a cool, dark place.

Nutrition Facts

Calories: 451 | Total Fat: 15.2g | Saturated Fat: 5g | Sodium: 1002mg

Carbohydrate: 2.9g | Sugars: 1.8g | Protein: 71g

Spiced Pork

Yield: 32 Servings

Preparation Time: 1-2 Hours (Excluding Canning Time)

Ingredients

- 16 pounds of pork loin, 1-inch pieces
- 1 teaspoon garlic powder
- 1 teaspoon black pepper, optional
- 4 teaspoons canning/pickling salt

Directions

1. Sterilize the canning jars.
2. Next, prepare a pressure canner according to the manufacturer's instructions.
3. Cut the pork loin into pieces measuring approximately ¾".
4. Season the pork with garlic powder and black pepper.
5. Pack each quart jar with around 2 pounds of pork pieces.
6. Leave a 1" headspace.
7. Put about ½ teaspoon of canning salt in each jar.
8. Use a paper towel dampened with vinegar to clean off the rim of each jar.
9. Remove air bubbles.
10. Place lids and rings on the jars, ensuring that the lids are centered. Finger-tighten the rings without over-tightening them.
11. Add the jars to the canner.
12. Let the canner process the pork, and adjust according to altitude.
13. After the processing time, turn off the heat.
14. Open the canner lid and carefully remove the jars.
15. Let the jars cool to room temperature, listening for the "ping" sound indicating the lids are sealing.
16. Once completely cooled, remove the rings and rinse the jars quickly.
17. Store it in a cool, dark place.

Nutrition Facts

Calories: 549 | Total Fat: 31.6g | Saturated Fat: 11.9g | Sodium: 141mg

Carbohydrate: 0.1g | Sugars: 0g | Protein: 62g

Onion Pork

Yield: 4 Servings

Preparation Time: 1-2 Hours (Excluding Canning Time)

Ingredients

- 2 pounds of pork shoulder
- 1 tablespoon onion powder
- Sea salt and black pepper to taste

Directions

1. Sterilize the canning jars.
2. Next, prepare a pressure canner according to the manufacturer's instructions.
3. Cut the raw pork meat into ½ to 1-inch pieces, ensuring to include some fat.
4. The fat will melt into jelly and aid in preserving the meat.
5. Season the pork with onion powder, sea salt, and ground black pepper to taste.
6. Pack the raw pork into the jars, leaving 1-inch of headspace.
7. Remove air bubbles.
8. Use a damp kitchen towel to wipe the rims of each jar and remove any residue.
9. Place the rubber lids on the jars and screw on the rings tightly to prevent water from spilling into the jars.
10. Following the manufacturer's instructions, put the canning jars in the prepared pressure canner.
11. Adjust the processing time and pressure based on your altitude.
12. Once the processing time is complete, carefully remove the jars from the canner.
13. Let the jars cool completely for 24 hours.
14. Check the seals and store them in a cool, dark place.

Nutrition Facts

Calories: 668 | Total Fat: 48.5g | Saturated Fat: 17.8g | Sodium: 155mg

Carbohydrate: 1.4g | Sugars: 0.6g | Protein: 53g

Mississippi Pork Roast

Yield: 20 Servings

Preparation Time: 1-2 Hours (Excluding Canning Time)

Ingredients

- 10 (1/2 pounds each) Pork shoulder, cut into 2-inch cubes
- 2 teaspoons kosher salt
- 2 teaspoons Fresh ground black pepper
- 1 large minced onion
- 14 cups Chicken broth
- 14 teaspoons Ranch seasoning mix
- 32 ounces of Pepperoncini, sliced

Directions

1. Sterilize the canning jars.
2. Next, prepare a pressure canner according to the manufacturer's instructions.
3. Cut the raw pork meat into ½ to 1-inch pieces, ensuring to include some fat.
4. Season the pork with sea salt and ground black pepper to taste.
5. Add minced onion into each jar and pack the raw pork into the jars, leaving 1-inch of headspace.
6. Add more sea salt, black pepper, onions, ranch seasoning mix, and pepperoncini to the pork. Cover with a piece of pork fat.
7. Use a damp kitchen towel to wipe the rims of each jar and remove any residue.
8. Place the rubber lids on the jars and screw on the rings tightly to prevent water from spilling into the jars.
9. Prepare a water bath and ensure all the jars are submerged.
10. Boil the water and then reduce the heat to a rolling simmer.
11. Let the jars simmer for 2-3 hours.
12. After 2-3 hours, remove the pot from the heat and let the water cool down slightly.
13. Next, remove the hot jars from the pot and place them on a cloth. Cover the jars with a kitchen towel and let them cool completely.
14. Once cooled, press each lid with your finger to ensure they are properly sealed. The lids should not move up or down.
15. Store the jars in the refrigerator and consume the preserved pork within a week.

Nutrition Facts: Calories: 291 | Total Fat: 16.3g | Saturated Fat: 5.7g | Sodium: 852mg

Carbohydrate: 1.5g | Sugars: 0.8g | Protein: 32.2g

Easy Canned Pork

Yield: 4 Servings

Preparation Time: 30-40 Minutes (Excluding Canning Time)

Ingredients

- 1-2 pounds of pork shoulder
- 1 large white onion, minced
- Sea salt
- ½ teaspoon of oregano
- ½ teaspoon of paprika
- Freshly ground black pepper to taste

Directions

1. Sterilize jars and prepare a pressure canner according to the manufacturer's instructions.
2. Cut the raw pork meat into ½ to 1-inch pieces, ensuring to include some fat. The fat will melt into jelly and aid in preserving the meat.
3. Season the pork with sea salt, oregano, paprika, and ground black pepper to taste. Add minced onion into each jar.
4. Pack the raw pork into the jars, leaving 1-inch of headspace.
5. Add more sea salt, black pepper, and onions to the pork. Cover with a piece of pork fat.
6. Use a damp kitchen towel to wipe the rims of each jar and remove any residue.
7. Place the rubber lids on the jars and screw on the rings tightly to prevent water from spilling into the jars.
8. Prepare a water bath and ensure all the jars are submerged.
9. Let it boil, then reduce the heat to maintain a rolling simmer.
10. Let the jars simmer for 2-3 hours.
11. After 2-3 hours, remove the pot from the heat and let the water cool down slightly.
12. Next, carefully remove the hot jars from the pot and place them on a cloth. Cover the jars with a kitchen towel and let them cool completely.
13. Once cooled, press each lid with your finger to ensure they are properly sealed.
14. Store the jars in the refrigerator and consume the preserved pork within a week.
15. Please refer to the note at the beginning of this post for information on preserving meat for longer periods using appropriate canning equipment.

Nutrition Facts: Calories: 333 | Total Fat: 24.3g | Saturated Fat: 8.9g | Sodium: 77mg
Carbohydrate: 0.3g | Sugars: 0g | Protein: 26.5g

Pork and Beans

Yield: 4 Servings

Preparation Time: 30 Minutes (Excluding Canning Time)

Ingredients

- 2 pounds navy or great Northern beans
- 3 cups water
- 4 cups of homemade tomato sauce
- 2 tablespoons honey
- 3/4 teaspoon prepared yellow mustard
- 1/4 cup brown sugar
- 2 medium onions chopped
- 1 1/2 - 3 tablespoons salt (optional)
- 8 pieces (2 inches) of bacon

Directions

1. Sterilize the canning jars.
2. Next, prepare a pressure canner according to the manufacturer's instructions.
3. Put the beans and enough water to cover by at least 2-3 inches in a large pot or gallon jar, and soak for 10 to 12 hours.
4. Rinse under tap water after soaking the beans for at least 12 hours.
5. In a sizable pot, place the beans and cover them with water. Heat the pot until it reaches a boiling point and allows the beans to boil for 30 minutes.
6. Add tomato sauce, honey, mustard, and brown sugar to a pot.
7. Heat the mixture until it reaches a boiling point while stirring frequently to ensure even distribution. It is important to continue stirring until the sugar is completely dissolved.
8. Using a canning funnel, evenly distribute the beans among the 8 jars. Aim for approximately 1/2 cup of beans in each jar.
9. Next, divide the onions equally among the jars, ensuring an even distribution.
10. Pour approximately one cup of sauce into each jar of beans and distribute it evenly.
11. Place 1 piece of salt pork or bacon in each jar, pushing it below the sauce.
12. Fill the jars with boiling water, leaving about 1-inch space at the top. Release any trapped air by using a thin knife or a bubble popper. If necessary, add more boiling water to fill the jars.
13. Use a damp kitchen towel to wipe the rim of each jar.
14. Secure the lids onto the jars and screw the rings on until they are finger-tight.
15. Following the manufacturer's instructions, put the canning jars in the prepared pressure canner.

16. Adjust the processing time and pressure based on your altitude.

17. Once the processing time is complete, carefully remove the jars from the canner.

18. Let the jars cool completely for 24 hours.

19. Check the seals and store them in a cool, dark place.

Nutrition Facts

Calories: 1100 | Total Fat: 19g | Saturated Fat: 6.1g | Sodium: 4828mg

Carbohydrate: 172.8g | Sugars: 33g | Protein: 67g

Pulled Pork

Yield: 10 Servings

Preparation Time: 20 Minutes (Excluding Canning Time)

Ingredients

- 5 pounds pork shoulder
- 2 tablespoons brown sugar
- 2 tablespoons paprika
- 1 tablespoon salt
- 1 tablespoon black pepper
- 1 tablespoon garlic powder
- 1 tablespoon onion powder
- 1 teaspoon cayenne pepper (optional)
- 1 cup barbecue sauce (your favorite brand or homemade)
- ½ cup apple cider vinegar

Directions

1. Cut the excess fat from the meat, and then cut it into several large pieces.
2. Mix the sugar, paprika, salt, pepper, garlic powder, onion powder, and (optional) cayenne pepper in a small bowl.
3. Mix well to create a dry rub.
4. Rub the dry rub mixture evenly over all sides of the pork pieces, coating them generously.
5. Place the seasoned pork pieces into a Dutch oven. Add the barbecue sauce and apple cider vinegar.
6. To prepare the pork, ensure it is covered in a Dutch oven.
7. Cook it on low heat for 12 hours.
8. Once the pork has been done, remove it from the Dutch oven and carefully transfer it to a big bowl or cutting board. Proceed to cut the pork into small bite-sized portions.
9. Cut the pork into smaller, bite-sized pieces.
10. While the pulled pork is still hot, pack it tightly into clean, sterilized canning jars, leaving about 1-inch of headspace.
11. Pour any remaining cooking liquid from the slow cooker or Dutch oven into a saucepan and bring it to a boil.
12. Carefully pour the boiling cooking liquid over the pulled pork in each jar, ensuring the liquid covers the meat and maintains the 1-inch headspace.
13. Remove air bubbles.

14. Clean the rims.

15. Place the canning lids on top of the jars and screw them.

16. Following the manufacturer's instructions, put the canning jars in the prepared pressure canner.

17. Adjust the processing time and pressure based on your altitude.

18. Once the processing time is complete, carefully remove the jars from the canner.

19. Let the jars cool completely for 24 hours.

20. Check the seals and store them in a cool, dark place.

Nutrition Facts

Calories: 720 | Total Fat: 48.8g | Saturated Fat: 17.9g | Sodium: 1134mg
Carbohydrate: 13.4g | Sugars: 8.9g | Protein: 53.3g

BBQ Minced Pork

Yield: 10 Servings

Preparation Time: 10 Minutes (Excluding Canning Time)

Ingredients

- 5 pounds of minced pork
- 2 teaspoons of salt
- 1 cup of BBQ sauce
- 1/4 cup of brown sugar
- 1 tablespoon of Worcestershire sauce
- 1 teaspoon of garlic powder
- 1/2 teaspoon of black pepper

Directions

1. Take a large mixing bowl and combine all the ingredients.
2. Pack the seasoned minced pork into pint-sized jars, leaving 1-inch of headspace.
3. Remove air bubbles.
4. Clean the jar rims with a damp cloth and place hot lids and bands on the jars.
5. Following the manufacturer's instructions, put the canning jars in the prepared pressure canner.
6. Adjust the processing time and pressure based on your altitude.
7. Once the processing time is complete, carefully remove the jars from the canner.
8. Let the jars cool completely for 24 hours.
9. Check the seals and store them in a cool, dark place.

Nutrition Facts

Calories: 378 | Total Fat: 8g | Saturated Fat: 2.7g | Sodium: 892mg

Carbohydrate: 13.2g | Sugars: 10.4g | Protein: 59.4g

Italian Minced Pork

Yield: 10 Servings

Preparation Time: 10 Minutes (Excluding Canning Time)

Ingredients

- 5 pounds of minced pork
- 2 teaspoons of salt
- 1 tablespoon of dried oregano
- 1 tablespoon of dried basil
- 1 teaspoon of garlic powder
- 1 teaspoon of onion powder
- 1/2 teaspoon of black pepper

Directions

1. Take a large mixing bowl, and combine all the ingredients in it.
2. Pack the seasoned minced pork into pint-sized jars, leaving 1-inch of headspace.
3. Remove air bubbles.
4. Clean the jar rims with a damp cloth and place hot lids and bands on the jars.
5. Following the manufacturer's instructions, put the canning jars in the prepared pressure canner.
6. Adjust the processing time and pressure based on your altitude.
7. Once the processing time is complete, carefully remove the jars from the canner.
8. Let the jars cool completely for 24 hours.
9. Check the seals and store them in a cool, dark place.

Nutrition Facts

Calories: 328 | Total Fat: 8g | Saturated Fat: 2.7g | Sodium: 595mg

Carbohydrate: 0.8g | Sugars: 0.2g | Protein: 59.5g

Pork Carnitas

Yield: 40 Servings

Preparation Time: 25 Minutes (Excluding Canning Time)

Ingredients

- 20 pounds Pork Shoulder, fat trimmed and cubed
- ¼ tablespoon Cumin
- ¼ tablespoon Canning Salt
- 1-inch Bay leaf
- ¼ tablespoon Onion powder
- 1/2 teaspoon Garlic powder
- 1/4 teaspoon Orange juice; Concentrate
- 1 teaspoon Oregano

Directions

1. Rub pork with all the listed ingredients and spices.
2. To begin, pack the pork into pint jars.
3. Remove air bubbles.
4. Place the hot lids and bands on the jars securely.
5. Following the manufacturer's instructions, put the canning jars in the prepared pressure canner.
6. Adjust the processing time and pressure based on your altitude.
7. Once the processing time is complete, carefully remove the jars from the canner.
8. Let the jars cool completely for 24 hours.
9. Check the seals and store them in a cool, dark place.

Nutrition Facts

Calories: 663 | Total Fat: 48.5g | Saturated Fat: 17.8g | Sodium: 190mg

Carbohydrate: 0.1g | Sugars: 0g | Protein: 52.8g

Pork And Leek Stew

Yield: 8 Servings

Preparation Time: 20 Minutes (Excluding Canning Time)

Ingredients

- 4 pounds of pork shoulder, cut into 1-inch pieces
- 4 cups leeks, sliced (white and light green parts only)
- 2 cloves garlic, minced
- 2 carrots, diced
- 2 potatoes, peeled and diced
- 2 cups chicken or vegetable broth
- 1 teaspoon dried thyme
- 1 teaspoon salt
- 1/2 teaspoon black pepper

Directions

1. Cook the pork pieces in a large pot over medium-high heat until brown.
2. Add the leeks, garlic, carrots, and potatoes to the pot.
3. Cook for 5 minutes, stirring occasionally.
4. Pour the chicken or vegetable broth and season with thyme, salt, and black pepper.
5. Stir to combine.
6. Let the mixture to a simmer and cook for another 5 minutes.
7. Transfer the stew into pint or quart jars, leaving 1-inch of headspace.
8. Remove air bubbles.
9. Clean the rims of the canning jars with a clean damp kitchen cloth.
10. Place the hot lids and screw on the band's fingertip tight.
11. Following the manufacturer's instructions, put the canning jars in the prepared pressure canner.
12. Adjust the processing time and pressure based on your altitude.
13. Once the processing time is complete, carefully remove the jars from the canner.
14. Let the jars cool completely for 24 hours.
15. Check the seals and store them in a cool, dark place.

Nutrition Facts

Calories: 787 | Total Fat: 49.8g | Saturated Fat: 18.2g | Sodium: 490mg
Carbohydrate: 16.6g | Sugars: 3.1g | Protein: 64.7g

Minced Pork

Yield: 10 Servings

Preparation Time: 15 Minutes (Excluding Canning Time)

Ingredients

- 5 pounds of minced pork
- 2 teaspoons of salt
- 1 tablespoon of paprika
- 1 tablespoon of chili powder
- 1 teaspoon of cayenne pepper
- 1 teaspoon of garlic powder
- 1 teaspoon of onion powder
- 1/2 teaspoon of black pepper

Directions

1. Take a large mixing bowl and combine all the ingredients and mix well.
2. Pack the seasoned minced pork into pint-sized jars, leaving 1-inch of headspace.
3. Remove air bubbles.
4. Clean the jar rims with a damp cloth and place hot lids and bands on the jars.
5. Following the manufacturer's instructions, put the canning jars in the prepared pressure canner.
6. Adjust the processing time and pressure based on your altitude.
7. Once the processing time is complete, carefully remove the jars from the canner.
8. Let the jars cool completely for 24 hours.
9. Check the seals and store them in a cool, dark place.

Nutrition Facts

Calories: 331 | Total Fat: 8.2g | Saturated Fat: 2.8g | Sodium: 602mg

Carbohydrate: 1.4g | Sugars: 0.3g | Protein: 59.6g

Sweet and Tangy Minced Pork

Yield: 10 Servings

Preparation Time: 15 Minutes (Excluding Canning Time)

Ingredients

- 1 cup of ketchup
- 1/2 cup of apple cider vinegar
- 1/4 cup of brown sugar
- 2 tablespoons of Worcestershire sauce
- 1 tablespoon of soy sauce
- 1 teaspoon of garlic powder
- 1/2 teaspoon of black pepper
- 5 pounds of minced pork
- 2 teaspoons of salt

Directions

1. Mix the ketchup, apple cider vinegar, brown sugar, Worcestershire sauce, soy sauce, garlic powder, and black pepper in a large mixing bowl.
2. Mix well to create the sauce.
3. Add the minced pork and salt to the sauce mixture. Mix thoroughly until the pork is evenly coated.
4. Pack the saucy minced pork into pint-sized jars, leaving 1-inch of headspace.
5. Remove air bubbles.
6. Clean the jar rims with a damp cloth and place hot lids and bands on the jars.
7. Following the manufacturer's instructions, put the canning jars in the prepared pressure canner.
8. Adjust the processing time and pressure based on your altitude.
9. Once the processing time is complete, carefully remove the jars from the canner.
10. Let the jars cool completely for 24 hours.
11. Check the seals and store them in a cool, dark place.

Nutrition Facts

Calories: 369 | Total Fat: 8g | Saturated Fat: 2.7g | Sodium: 987mg

Carbohydrate: 10.1g | Sugars: 7.3g | Protein: 61.8g

Tomato Pork

Yield: 10 Servings

Preparation Time: 15 Minutes (Excluding Canning Time)

Ingredients

- 5 pounds of pork, diced
- 4 cups of tomato sauce
- 2 cups of diced tomatoes
- 1 cup of chopped onions
- 1 cup of chopped bell peppers
- 4 cloves of garlic, minced
- 2 teaspoons of salt
- 1 teaspoon of dried oregano
- 1/2 teaspoon of black pepper

Directions

1. In a large pot, combine the tomato sauce, diced tomatoes, onions, bell peppers, garlic, salt, oregano, and black pepper. Mix well.
2. Add the diced pork to the tomato mixture and mix to coat it well.
3. Heat the mixture over low heat until it starts to simmer. Let it simmer for 10 minutes.
4. Pack the pork and tomato sauce mixture into pint-sized jars, leaving 1-inch headspace.
5. Remove air bubbles.
6. Clean the jar rims with a damp cloth.
7. Place hot lids and bands on the jars.
8. Following the manufacturer's instructions, put the canning jars in the prepared pressure canner.
9. Adjust the processing time and pressure based on your altitude.
10. Once the processing time is complete, carefully remove the jars from the canner.
11. Let the jars cool completely for 24 hours.
12. Check the seals and store them in a cool, dark place.

Nutrition Facts

Calories: 365 | Total Fat: 8.3g | Saturated Fat: 2.8g | Sodium: 1111mg

Carbohydrate: 9.2g | Sugars: 6.2g | Protein: 61.3g

Worcestershire Pork

Yield: 10 Servings

Preparation Time: 15 Minutes (Excluding Canning Time)

Ingredients

- 5 pounds of pork shoulder or pork loin, diced
- 1 cup Worcestershire sauce
- 1/2 cup soy sauce
- 1/4 cup brown sugar

- 2 tablespoons apple cider vinegar
- 1 tablespoon minced garlic
- 1 tablespoon onion powder
- 1 teaspoon black pepper
- 1/2 teaspoon paprika

Directions

1. Combine Worcestershire sauce, soy sauce, brown sugar, apple cider vinegar, minced garlic, onion powder, black pepper, and paprika in a large bowl. Mix well to create a marinade.
2. Add the diced pork to the marinade and toss to coat evenly.
3. Prepare your pressure canner and jars according to the manufacturer's instructions.
4. Transfer the marinated pork and the marinade into pint-sized jars, leaving 1-inch of headspace.
5. Remove air bubbles.
6. Clean the jar rims with a damp cloth and place hot lids and bands on the jars.
7. Process the jars in your pressure canner according to altitude.
8. Adjust the processing time and pressure based on your altitude.
9. Once the processing time is complete, carefully remove the jars from the canner.
10. Let the jars cool completely for 24 hours.
11. Check the seals and store them in a cool, dark place.

Nutrition Facts

Calories: 599 | Total Fat: 31.6g | Saturated Fat: 11.9g | Sodium: 1125mg

Carbohydrate: 10.4g | Sugars: 8.8g | Protein: 62.9g

Pork and Corn Stew

Yield: 8 Servings

Preparation Time: 20 Minutes (Excluding Canning Time)

Ingredients

- 4 pounds of pork shoulder, cut into 1-inch pieces
- 1 large onion, chopped
- 2 cloves garlic, minced
- 2 cups fresh or frozen corn kernels
- 2 tablespoons Worcestershire sauce
- 1 teaspoon salt
- 1/2 teaspoon black pepper
- 2 cups chicken or beef broth

Directions

1. In a large pot, brown pork pieces on each side over medium-high heat.
2. Put the onions and garlic and cook for 5 minutes.
3. Add corn, Worcestershire sauce, salt, and black pepper.
4. Stir to combine.
5. Add in broth and bring it to a simmer.
6. Transfer mixture to pint or quart jars, leaving 1-inch of headspace.
7. Remove air bubbles.
8. Process the jars in your pressure canner according to altitude.
9. Adjust the processing time and pressure based on your altitude.
10. Once the processing time is complete, carefully remove the jars from the canner.
11. Let the jars cool completely for 24 hours.
12. Check the seals and store them in a cool, dark place.

Nutrition Facts

Calories: 761 | Total Fat: 49.9g | Saturated Fat: 18.2g | Sodium: 510mg

Carbohydrate: 10.7g | Sugars: 2.8g | Protein: 64.3g

Pork and Corn Salsa

Yield: 4 Servings

Preparation Time: 20-30 Minutes (Excluding Canning Time)

Ingredients

- 2 pounds of pork tenderloin, cubed into 1-inch pieces
- 2 cups fresh or frozen corn kernels
- 2 large tomatoes, chopped
- 1 large red onion, chopped
- 1/2 cup chopped fresh cilantro
- 1 jalapeno pepper, seeded and minced
- 2 tablespoons lime juice
- 1/2 teaspoon salt

Directions

1. In a large pot, brown pork pieces on all sides over medium-high heat.
2. Add corn, tomatoes, red onion, cilantro, jalapeno pepper, lime juice, and salt. Stir to combine.
3. Simmer the mixture for 10-15 minutes.
4. Transfer mixture to pint or quart jars, leaving 1-inch of headspace.
5. Process the jars in your pressure canner according to altitude.
6. Adjust the processing time and pressure based on your altitude.
7. Once the processing time is complete, carefully remove the jars from the canner.
8. Let the jars cool completely for 24 hours.
9. Check the seals and store them in a cool, dark place.

Nutrition Facts

Calories: 429 | Total Fat: 8.8g | Saturated Fat: 2.8g | Sodium: 428mg
Carbohydrate: 25g | Sugars: 7g | Protein: 62.8g

Polish Canned Pork

Yield: 16 Servings

Preparation Time: 20-30 Minutes (Excluding Canning Time)

Ingredients

- 8 pounds of pork loin, shoulder
- 2 tablespoons of salt
- 1 tablespoon of dried marjoram
- 1 teaspoon of black pepper
- 12 tablespoons of lard

Directions

1. Begin by washing the pork thoroughly.
2. Cut it into small, uniform pieces, about ½ inches x ½ inches (1.5 cm x 1.5 cm) in size.
3. Combine the diced pork with salt, dried marjoram, and black pepper in a bowl. Mix well to distribute the seasonings evenly. Place the mixture in the refrigerator and let it marinate overnight.
4. Sterilize the canning jars.
5. Pack the marinated pork tightly into each sterilized jar, filling them about three-quarters full. Ensure there is enough room for the lard and proper sealing.
6. Then, add 1 tablespoon of lard on top of the pork in each jar.
7. The lard helps preserve the meat and adds flavor.
8. Remove air bubbles.
9. Seal the jars tightly with their lids, ensuring a proper seal to prevent leakage.
10. Process the jars in a pressure canner.
11. Adjust the processing time and pressure based on your altitude.
12. Once the processing time is complete, carefully remove the jars from the canner.
13. Let the jars cool completely for 24 hours.
14. Check the seals and store them in a cool, dark place.

Nutrition Facts: Calories: 636 | Total Fat: 41.2g | Saturated Fat: 15.6g | Sodium: 1013mg
Carbohydrate: 0.2g | Sugars: 0g | Protein: 62g

Raw Pack Pork

Yield: 4 Servings

Preparation Time: 20-30 Minutes (Excluding Canning Time)

Ingredients

- 2 pounds of Fresh pork, trimmed and cut into 1-inch pieces
- Canning salt (optional)

Directions

1. Prepare your canner and sterilize canning jars, lids, and bands according to the manufacturer's instructions.
2. Fill each sterilized jar with raw pork pieces or cubes, leaving about 1-inch headspace.
3. Add 1/2 teaspoon of canning salt to each jar (optional) if desired.
4. Gently shake the jars to settle the pork and remove any air bubbles. Use a non-metallic utensil to release any trapped air if necessary.
5. Wipe the rim with a damp cloth.
6. Put the sterilized lids on the jars and screw the bands.
7. Carefully place the filled jars into the canner.
8. Process the jars in the canner at the recommended pressure and time for your altitude and jar size. The processing time will vary based on the size of the jar and your specific canner. Consult a reliable canning resource or recipe for precise processing time and pressure.
9. After the canner has depressurized and is safe to open, carefully remove the jars using canning jar lifters. Place them on a heat-resistant surface or a towel-lined countertop.
10. Let the jars cool.
11. Check the seals and store them in a cool, dark place.

Nutrition Facts: Calories: 324 | Total Fat: 8g | Saturated Fat: 2.7g | Sodium: 249mg
Carbohydrate: 0g | Sugars: 0g | Protein: 59.4g

INDEX

Conversion Chart

Spoons

16 tablespoons	1 cup
1 tablespoon	1/16 cup
12 tablespoons	3/4 cup
2 tablespoons	1/8 cup
10 tablespoons	2/3 cup
4 tablespoons	1/4 cup
5 tablespoons	1/3 cup
8 tablespoons	1/2 cup

Temperatures

°C	°F
200	390
210	410
220	430
230	445
240	464
250	482

Volume: Liquid Conversion

Metric	Imperial	USA
250ml	8 fl ounces	1 cup
150ml	5 fl ounces	2/3 cup
120ml	4 fl oz	1/2 cup
75ml	2 1/2 fl ounces	1/3 cup
60ml	2 fl ounces	1/4 cup
15ml	1/2 fl ounces	1 tablespoon
180ml	6 fl ounces	3/4 cup

Weight		
Grams	**Ounces**	**Cups**
15	0.5	
25	0.9	
50	1.8	
75	2.6	0.33
100	3.5	
150	5.3	0.67
175	6.2	
200	7.1	
225	7.9	1
250	8.8	
275	9.7	
300	10.6	1.33
350	12.3	
375	13.2	1.67
400	14.1	1.75
425	15	
450	15.9	2
500	17.6	
700	24.7	
750	26.5	3
1000	35.3	
1250	44.1	5.5
1500	52.9	
2000	70.5	9

Pressure Canning Meat, Vegetables, Fish, Seafood, Soup: Altitude And Pressure Chart				
Altitude feet / meters	Weighted Gauge lb	Dial Gauge lb	Weighted Gauge kPa	Dial Gauge kPa
0 - 1000 / 0 - 305	10	11	69	76
1001 - 2000 / 306 - 609	15	11	103	76
2001 - 4000 / 610 - 1219	15	12	103	83
4001 - 6000 / 1220 - 1828	15	13	103	90
6001 - 8000 / 1829 - 2438	15	14	103	97
8001 - 10000 / 2439 - 3048	15	15	103	103

GET YOR BONUS NOW

SCAN THE QR CODE

Or go to the link:

https://emma-yoder.aweb.page/p/025cddfb-5732-4ab3-a6a0-4c0aaa2cd185

Made in the USA
Las Vegas, NV
10 July 2023

74426539R00087